Text by Angie Belcher
Edited by Anna Tyler
Photography by Andy Belcher
Series Editor: Tony Halliday

POCKET GUIDE

Fiji

First Edition 2007

PHOTOGRAPHY
All photography by Andy Belcher except pages 14 Mary Evans Picture Library; 17 Alinari/Topfoto; 18 Topfoto; 21 AFP/Getty Images.
Cover photograph: Douglas Peebles Photography/Alamy

CONTACTING THE EDITORS
Every effort has been made to provide accurate information in this publication, but changes are inevitable. The publisher cannot be responsible for any resulting loss, inconvenience or injury. We would appreciate it if readers would call our attention to any errors or outdated information by contacting Berlitz Publishing, PO Box 7910, London SE1 1WE, England.
Fax: (44) 20 7403 0290
Email: berlitz@apaguide.co.uk
<www.berlitzpublishing.com>

Printed in Singapore by Insight Print Services (Pte) Ltd, 38 Joo Koon Road, Singapore 628990.
Tel: (65) 6865-1600. Fax: (65) 6861-6438

Berlitz Trademark Reg. U.S. Patent Office and other countries. Marca Registrada

➤ **Raft the hidden valleys of the Upper Navua River (page 48) and see part of the wild interior of Viti Levu**

By car, bus or train, tour the Coral Coast of Viti Levu (page 42), passing sugar-cane fields, beaches, resorts and coral-fringed lagoons ◄

Find out about traditional Fijian society and culture at the Pacific Harbour Arts Village (page 47), Viti Levu ▼

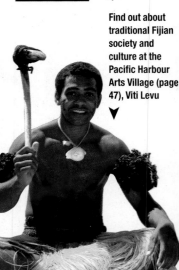

TOP TEN ATTRACTIONS

Cruise through or stay on the Yasawas (page 32), a string of islands encircled by white-sand beaches

With its coral reefs and clear water, Fiji has some of the world's best diving and snorkelling (page 81)

Hear the sounds of the islands: listen to a *meke* (page 92) or attend a Sunday church service

Kava, much more than just a drink, is central to an elaborate social ritual (page 105)

On Taveuni, trek to see the waterfalls of Bouma National Heritage Park (page 74)

Laze on an isolated beach and enjoy the feeling peace and relaxation

Visit the lovely village of Navala (page 39), in the Nausori Highlands, with its thatched-roof *bures*

CONTENTS

Fact Sheets

INTRODUCTION

Ask any visitor to Fiji what they remember most about their stay, and they'll probably say the people. Fijians combine a ready humour with a slow, relaxed manner, and their curiosity, confidence and connections to historical customs create a unique culture and the ideal holiday atmosphere. Add to this a generous helping of tropicana – balmy nights and palm trees, deserted beaches lapped by tepid and crystal-clear waters, the old colonial towns and wild rainforests – and you have all the ingredients for a truly unforgettable island holiday.

At the Heart of the Pacific

The Fijian archipelago is extensive, comprising some 330 islands (of which 100 or so are inhabited) spread over 1.3 million sq km (502,000 sq miles) of the southwest Pacific Ocean. The country is located roughly in the middle of the Pacific, 2,798km (1,739 miles) northeast of Sydney, Australia, and 1,848km (1,148 miles) north of Auckland, New Zealand. Its neightbours in the Pacific are Tonga, to the east, and Vanuatu, to the west. Fiji's central location has made it a focal point for travellers and traders for many years.

The two main islands are Viti Levu and Vanua Levu. Viti Levu, the largest, has an area of 10,400 sq km (3,950 sq miles) and accounts for more than half of Fiji's total land area. It is Fiji's most highly populated island – most Fijians live there. The second-largest island, Vanua Levu, lies northeast of Viti Levu and is just over half the size, with an area of around 5,500 sq km (2,000 sq miles).

To the east of Vanua Levu, separated by the Somosomo Strait, is Taveuni, the third-largest island, around the same

Palm-tree fun, Taveuni

size as Kadavu, which lies south of Viti Levu. Other small clusters of islands are divided into groups: Lomaiviti (just off the east coast of Viti Levu), Lau (well to the east, towards Tonga), the Mamanucas (just off the west coast) and the Yasawas (to the north of the Mamanucas).

The international airport, located at Nadi on the western side of Viti Levu, is the main hub for flights from abroad and to domestic and other Pacific destinations. The capital, Suva, lies at the southeastern end of Viti Levu and is the nation's largest city and major port.

Most of the Fijian islands are either of volcanic origin, with sharp, mountainous ridges, or of coral and limestone, with white-sand beaches, shallow fringing reefs and some rocky outcrops. On the larger islands, wind patterns and topography have combined to produce a marked difference in vegetation between the lush eastern sides and the western sides, which can be desolate, dry areas with poor vegetation.

The islands are located in the path of the southeast trade winds, and are swept by steady breezes from the east throughout the year. Occasional cyclones and hurricanes occur between November and March. Temperatures vary little throughout the day or at various times of the year.

Tabua

The *tabua* (pronounced 'tam-bua') is the tooth of a sperm whale, and to receive one is a mark of great honour and respect. Presented to chiefs at important conferences, especially those debating war or peace, *tabua* were used to seal contracts or reconcile differences. Nowadays they are more likely to be presented to visiting dignitaries, or passed between families to show sympathy, request a favour, or when a marriage is arranged. *Tabua* are not meant to be bought or sold, but passed from family to family or from tribe to tribe.

Getting ready to sail, Lau Group

An Island Nation

Fiji's population of just over 785,000 is comprised of nearly equal numbers of indigenous Fijians (49.9 percent) and Indians (46.2 percent), the latter being descendants of indentured labourers brought from India by the British in the late 1800s to work in the sugar-cane fields. The ethnic mixture is reflected in the religions practised in Fiji: the islands are dotted with Christian churches, mosques, and Sikh and Hindu temples.

Native Fijians are descendants of Melanesian seafarers who settled the islands more than 3,500 years ago. Most live in village communities comprising extended family groups known as *mataqali*. Each *mataqali* owns land in common and belongs to a broader group or clan that is subject to a paramount chief. Clans gather from across great distances for major social events which involve the exchange of gifts and huge communal feasts cooked in underground ovens *(lovo)*. These colourful spectacles embrace singing, dancing and the retelling of

**Indo-Fijian mother
and daughter**

ancient stories of Fijian migration, wars and mortality. Of great importance in this culture is kava. It sometimes seems that everything that matters in Fiji is discussed around a *tanoa* (kava bowl), and few meetings or gatherings take place without the kava ceremony taking place.

A majority of the Indian population is concentrated in the cane-growing areas, in small settlements or towns. They are hard-working, thrifty and efficient entrepreneurs who dominate Fiji's commercial centres. Their high profile in the retail sector has lead to a distorted perception of their wealth and position, and has been attributed as the cause of a degree of racial disharmony in urban areas.

Smaller ethnic groups include Europeans, Chinese and other Pacific Islanders. Among the first Europeans to make lives for themselves in Fiji were shipwrecked sailors in the early 19th century. Opportunities for economic gain later attracted businessmen and planters, and by 1870 the white population was estimated at around 2,000. It continued to grow until it reached a peak in the 1960s of around 7,000, falling away after Fiji gained independence in 1970. There are now about 4,200 Europeans. Over the years, Europeans have intermarried with Fijians. These *kai loma* (part-Europeans) live happily with a foot in both worlds.

The Chinese arrived in the early 20th century and, like the Indians, show a strong entrepreneurial spirit. Pacific Islanders include Tongans, Samoans and the descendants of Solomon Islanders taken to Fiji as labourers in the 19th century.

Garden Islands

Fiji has a well-earned reputation for the beauty of its tropical vegetation. Colourful poinciana (flame trees) and bougainvillea border the roads, while the slightest of breezes will waft the fragrance of frangipani on the air. Vast, almost impenetrable rainforests cover the windward slopes of the main islands – Taveuni's forests hide the rare and beautiful tagimaucia flower – and coconut plantations abound along the coastal plains. Crops of sugar cane are cultivated on the lowlands

Darkening this picture is the fact that a quarter of Fiji's surviving native forests – which cover 40 percent of the land area – are classified as suitable for logging. Already the massive dakua (kauri) tree – once carved into war canoes – has vanished from Viti Levu, and the last stands on Vanua Levu are now being logged. The establishment of national parks and reserves offers some protection to the most threatened areas.

Delicate native flowers

With 70 species of land birds, 22 of which are endemic, the islands are a paradise for birdwatchers. Introduced species like the loud, cheeky mynah from India make their presence known, and red and green kula (collared lories) compete with other species for the nectar and pollen from flowering trees.

The only native mammals are small insect-eating bats

The Fijian people value their wildlife. Some clans have totemic relationships with eels, prawns, turtles and sharks. In some places ancient chants and rituals are still used to summon these creatures. Red prawns are 'called' on Vatulele, sharks in southern Lau and eels near Korolevu. Sea turtles are summoned on Kadavu and Koro, although these marine reptiles are becoming rare.

and the monkey-faced fruit bat or flying fox, large numbers of which can be seen at dusk. Geckos and skinks are prolific, and the large, forest-dwelling banded iguana can reach 70cm (28in) in length.

The islands' garden-like terrain extends beneath the sea to the coral reefs, which thrive thanks to warm seas, copious amounts of sunlight, nutrient-rich waters and the circulation of cleansing waters by tidal and wind-driven currents. It's thanks to the reefs, and their rich diversity of marine life, that Fiji has some of the world's best diving. Great Astrolable Reef, Rainbow Reef and the Great White Wall are found on almost every list of the world's most memorable dive sites.

But it's not only the diving that attracts visitors: Fiji also has surfing, hiking, white-water rafting, rock climbing, horse trekking and kayaking to tempt visitors. Nature-lovers will discover dense, damp tropical rainforests whose deep silence is broken only by the calls of exotic birds, and by the sound of waterfalls cascading into deep, dark pools. Honeymooners find romance on isolated beaches, while those interested in history may explore the ruins of a pre-European hill fortification or wander through a colonial town. From big-game fishing to hand-line fishing, and whether you prefer lazing in the luxury of a seaside villa or bathing in beams of sunlight that filter through a *bure* shutter, Fiji is an antidote to the everyday stresses of modern living.

A BRIEF HISTORY

Fijians would have to be one of the friendliest people in the world, so it's hard to comprehend that any narration of their history includes cannibalism, tribal warfare, colonial exploitation and military coups.

Little is known of the islanders' history before the arrival of Europeans, but archaeological finds suggest that the first inhabitants were the Lapita people, who arrived from Melanesia around 3,500 years ago. Evidence of their settlement exists throughout Fiji. Skeletal remains from that era have been found in the Sigatoka Sand Dunes. Stone mounds and circular foundations in some remote areas suggest the establishment of fortified villages, but any remains of ancient wood or thatch dwellings have long succumbed to the tropical climate.

Traditional village, Navala

Fijians firewalking

The Lapita were followed by more migrants from Melanesia, who made permanent settlements from around 500BC. Tongan warriors from Polynesia arrived around AD1000; the Tongan influence is still strong in the Lau island group.

European Arrival

Seafarers of the 17th and 18th centuries were the first Europeans to record the existence of this group of islands. The Dutch explorer Abel Tasman sighted Fiji in 1643, and the English navigator Captain James Cook visited one of the southernmost islands in 1774.

Captain William Bligh followed in 1789 after the mutiny on the *Bounty*. Bligh and loyal crew members had been set adrift in a longboat by the mutineers. Bligh sailed the craft through the Fijian islands, passing between Viti Levu and Vanua Levu and narrowly escaping capture by a Fijian war canoe. The islands were known for some time as the Bligh Islands, and the stretch of water between them is still called Bligh Water.

Given the treacherous nature of Fiji's reefs, and accounts of fierce warriors and cannibalism – Fiji became known as the 'Cannibal Isles' – many early voyagers judiciously avoided the islands. The first European settlers were shipwrecked sailors. In 1800, the American schooner *Argo* ran aground on a reef near Lakeba (Lau Group). Most of the crew made it safely to land, but were then either killed by Fijians or died of the cholera that had broken out on board. Cholera was also contracted by the Fijians, who had no resistance to European diseases, and the epidemic soon spread to Lakeba and other islands, killing thousands of people.

A sailor by the name of Oliver Slater managed to survive both cholera and the cooking pot, and established a workable relationship with the islanders. This was to spell doom to the healthy stands of sandalwood that grew in such abundance along the Bua coast of Vanua Levu.

The sandalwood trade was then controlled by the Tongans, who would obtain it from the chiefs and sell it to the Europeans. When Slater made his way to Australia, the news he spread of the highly prized timber had a devastating impact on the environment and the people. Between 1804 and 1813 a rush of traders and beachcombers arrived on the islands, trading guns, ammunition and tobacco directly with the Fijians until little of the timber remained. As a by-product, the introduction of European weapons led to an escalation of violent warfare between tribes.

A Brutal Past

The early Fijians adhered to a strict system of rituals and taboos which controlled their day-to-day existence. Even minor violations of the laws were punishable by death, and important events called for human sacrifice. When chiefs or honoured warriors died, their wives were killed or buried alive with them. Cannibalism was practised. Wars were frequent and accompanied by great cruelty; prisoners of war were tortured and eaten. War canoes were often launched on ramps made up of live people. Fijians who volunteered to hold the corner posts when new temples or houses for their rulers were being built could find themselves buried alive and supporting them.

The next of Fiji's natural products to be exploited was the bêche-de-mer, or sea cucumber. Smoked and dried, it fetched a good price in China, and the trade continued until the 1850s.

The Struggle for Power

Traders and settlers established the first European-style town, Levuka, on Ovalau, in the early 1820s; but the real power lay on Bau, off the east coast of Viti Levu. Trade with the Europeans had been most intense in Bau, resulting in a great accumulation of wealth and power by the ruling Bauan chief, Cakobau, also know as Tui Viti, or 'King of Fiji'.

In 1848 a Tongan noble, Enele Ma'afu, led a fleet of war canoes to capture Vanua Balavu in northern Lau. He became governor of all Tongans in Lau and by 1854 was a serious threat to Cakobau's power. From the late 1850s the Tongans were the controlling force in eastern Fiji.

Ma'afu brought in Wesleyan missionaries from Tonga, and Christianity was slowly accepted as the Fijians identified similarities with their own beliefs, for example the concepts of *tabu* (sacred prohibition) and *mana* (spiritual power). This gave the Methodist Church a foothold in Fiji. In the 1830s the missionaries arrived in southern Lau. Cakobau eventually converted to Christianity in 1854.

By the 1830s the settlement at Levuka had grown to be the major port of call for traders and warships in the South Pacific, and in 1840 Commandant Charles Wilkes led a US expedition that produced the first chart of the Fijian islands. He also negotiated a treaty in which the chiefdom of Bau was paid to protect foreign ships and supply provisions.

But in 1841 relationships between the two groups began to deteriorate, when Levuka was ravaged by fires that settlers suspected were instigated by Cakobau. In 1849 the home of US Consul John Brown Williams was destroyed by fire. Williams held Cakobau responsible and sent him a bill for damages.

In 1862 Cakobau was under increasing financial pressure, and proposed to the British Consul that he would cede the islands to Queen Victoria in return for full settlement of his debts. The British thought this over for four years – then turned him down; but the rumours of British possession encouraged a large influx of settlers to Levuka, who brought all kinds of problems with them. Disputes erupted with Fijians over land ownership, and Levuka became a lawless outpost, always on the verge of anarchy and racial war.

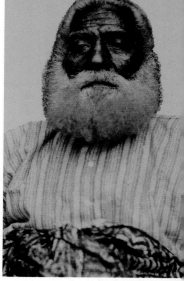

Chief Cakobau

Cakobau's debts were not cleared until 1868, when the Australian Polynesia Company agreed to pay them in exchange for 200,000 acres (80,000 hectares) of land to be used for plantations after the price of cotton skyrocketed during the American Civil War. The cotton boom stimulated 'blackbirding' – the slave trade. Labourers were brought to Fiji from the Solomon Islands and New Hebrides (Vanuatu), enticed into working for three years in return for minimal wages, food, clothing and a return passage home. (During the same period, Fijians were captured and forced to work on sugar plantations in Queensland, Australia.) Britain later stopped the trade after allegations of atrocities and abuse by recruiters. Cotton proved to be uneconomical on Fiji, and the plantations were replanted with coconut palms and sugar cane.

A council of chiefs met in 1865 in an attempt to form a national government, but did not succeed. Regional governments were formed in Bau (headed by Cakobau) and in Lau (run by Ma'afu). These went some way to establishing a sense of order, but led to no significant political reform. Hopes were high that the Cakobau government would pull it off; but trying to satisfy the differing needs of merchants, planters and Fijians proved too difficult. The government was unpopular, and there was talk of a race war. In order to ward off anarchy, Cakobau was forced to cede Fiji to Britain. The Deed of Cession was signed on 10 October 1874 in Nasova, near Levuka, and Fiji became a crown colony.

The Fijians continued to suffer from the European diseases that arrived with the settlers, and in 1875 a measles epidemic killed 40,000 Fijians, drastically reducing the number of workers needed to operate the plantations.

A 19th-century view of Ovalau

British Involvement

Sir Arthur Gordon, the colony's first governor, discouraged the use of 'natives' to work on plantations. He took steps to protect Fijians from being exploited as a labour force, and made it illegal to sell native land. He also established a taxation system which required Fijians to work their own land rather than that of any planter.

The laws established by Gordon safeguarded Fijians from the risk of becoming alienated from their land, or exploited as labourers. But the plantation crops still needed large pools of cheap labour. Between 1879 and 1919 some 60,000 contract workers from India arrived in Fiji, changing the cultural mix of the islands for ever. The agreement was that the workers could either settle in Fiji or return to India at their own cost after five years of labour. (Those who worked on the plantations for another five years were given free transport home.) About two-thirds of the contract workers decided to remain. The Indians had a high birth rate, the Fijians a high death rate, for they still fell victim to the European diseases to which Indians were acclimatised after two centuries of colonial rule in India. Eventually the Indian population exceeded that of the Fijians, while cultural and religious differences kept the two groups apart.

Restricted from buying Fijian land, the Indians moved into small business or took out long-term leases as independent farmers. The year 1920 saw the first major struggle by Indians for better conditions, and there was increasing labour unrest. By allying themselves with Fijian claims, the Europeans diverted attention from their own monopoly on freehold land and their power and influence in the civil service. It was convenient to blame all problems on the Indian community, and to exacerbate fears that the Indians were 'taking over'.

There was some minor involvement of Fijians in World War I, but World War II saw over 8,000 Fijians recruited to help stop the advancing Japanese in the Solomon Islands.

Independence

By the 1960s Fiji was moving towards self-government after nearly 100 years of colonial administration. The country finally achieved independence on 10 October 1970, with the British monarch as its head of state, represented in Fiji by a governor-general. Left unresolved were the issues of leases and land ownership, and how to deal with the competing interests of the two main ethnic groups.

The Fijian Alliance Party (FAP) won the first post-independence election and continued to govern without major interruption for the next 17 years. In the 1980s the price of sugar began to decline, Fiji's foreign debt escalated, the economy deteriorated and there was a heightening of ethnic tensions. Indo-Fijians were perceived as obsessed with making money and monopolising commerce. In reality they were no better-off than the indigenous Fijians, and unlike them, had no opportunity to secure land tenure on their farming leases.

In 1987 the Fiji Labour Party (FLP) was elected in coalition with the National Federation Party (NFP). Although the government had an indigenous Fijian prime minister and a Cabinet comprising an indigenous Fijian majority, it was still labelled Indian-dominated because most of its MPs were Indo-Fijian.

A Period of Instability

The victory of the coalition increased racial tensions. The extremist Taukei Movement played on Fijian fears of losing land rights, and of political and economic domination by Indo-Fijians. Lieutenant Colonel Sitiveni Rabuka led a bloodless coup in May 1987 and formed an interim civil government. In September 1987 Rabuka intervened again, and Fiji was declared a republic, with Rabuka as self-appointed head of state.

The coup had dire economic consequences. Two major sources of income, tourism and sugar, were drastically affected; developmental aid was suspended; and between 1987 and

1992 50,000 skilled and professional workers emigrated.

In July 1990 a new constitution was proclaimed that diminished the position of Indo-Fijians in the government. Indo-Fijian political leaders opposed the constitution, claiming that it was racist and undemocratic. Nevertheless, Rabuka was elected twice as prime minister, in 1992 and 1994.

A new constitution was declared in 1997. The position of president was reserved for an indigenous Fijian, but no provision was made for the ethnicity of the prime minister.

Commodore Bainimarama

In May 1999 voters rejected Rabuka and his party. The FLP won most seats, and its leader, Mahendra Chaudhry, became the country's first Indo-Fijian prime minister. Many indigenous Fijians were not pleased, fearing that their traditional land rights were at stake. On 19 May 2000 armed men led by George Speight, a bankrupt businessman, took over the parliamentary compound in Suva and held 30 hostages, including Chaudhry. He demanded the resignation of Chaudhry and President Ratu Sir Kamisese Mara, and the repeal of the 1997 multi-ethnic constitution.

In an attempt to resolve the situation, President Ratu Mara reluctantly announced that he was removing Chaudhry from power. Speight's group then demanded Mara's resignation. Commodore Frank Bainimarama, the head of Fiji's military, declared martial law. Eventually, the hostages were released and the 1997 constitution revoked. There was widespread international disapproval of these events. Tourism was badly affected, and many businesses collapsed.

In 2001 the appeal court upheld the 1997 constitution and ruled that Fiji take to the polls to restore democracy. Lasenia Qarase, heading the Fijian People's Party (SLD), won 32 of the 71 seats in the 2001 elections. Claiming that a multi-party Cabinet would not work under present circumstances, Qarase failed to include any FLP members in his 18-strong Cabinet.

Slowly Fiji began to rebuild confidence in the economy and in the country as a tourist destination, but racial tensions continued to simmer. The Qarase government's draft Promotion of Reconciliation, Tolerance and Unity Bill divided the country in 2004 and 2005. Supporters believed that the bill would help heal the rifts left by the last coup. Opponents feared that its provision for amnesty would pardon those involved in the coup.

In early 2006 tension between the government and the military, which opposed the bill, began to escalate. In December of that year, Commodore Bainimarama forced the government to resign. He later declared himself interim prime minister.

Island smile

Although the military is still in power, the situation today is calm and generally safe. After a slump caused by the events of December 2006, tourism has started to take off again. Today, visitors can expect to receive a friendly *'Bula!'* ('Hello!') wherever they go in these enchanting islands.

Historical Landmarks

1500BC Lapita seafarers arrive.

500BC Further Melanesian settlers arrive, probably from nearby Vanuatu or the Solomon Islands.

AD1000 Polynesians arrive from Tonga.

1643 Abel Tasman is the first European to sail through the islands.

1774 James Cook anchors in the Lau Group. Fiji becomes known as the 'Cannibal Islands'.

1789 William Bligh charts parts of the islands, but is chased off by canoes in the Yasawas.

1804 A shipwrecked survivor finds sandalwood, leading to an influx of European traders.

1830s Missionaries arrive to convert the islanders to Christianity.

1860s–1870s The era of 'blackbirding': islanders from the Solomons and Vanuatu are coerced into working on plantations in Fiji; Fijians are coerced into working on plantations in Queensland, Australia.

1874 (10 October) Fiji becomes a British colony.

1879 The British begin to bring Indians to Fiji to work on sugar cane, coconut and cotton plantations.

1919 Indian immigration ends.

1963 Fiji holds its first general election.

1970 (10 October) Fiji gains independence from Britain.

1987 In May, Lieutenant Colonel Sitiveni Rabuka overthrows the Fijian government. In September, Fiji becomes a republic.

1992 Fiji holds its first general election under a new constitution.

1999 Fiji gains its first Indian prime minister, Mahendra Chaudry.

2000 A coup led by George Speight overthrows the elected government. The president steps down and a military government takes over until a new civilian government is formed.

2005 The Qarase government's draft Promotion of Reconciliation, Tolerance and Unity Bill divides the country.

2006 Political unrest. The nation's military chief, Commodore Frank Bainimarama, leads a bloodless coup.

WHERE TO GO

I t would be easy to arrive in Fiji, settle into the laid-back, languid pace of the Pacific and idle away the days. And there's nothing wrong with that. But to really experience Fiji you need time.

Time for your senses to absorb the experience of cool spray from cascading waterfalls, hot sand on crescent-shaped beaches and tepid waters in blue lagoons. Time to smell the smoking *lovo* (food prepared in an underground oven), and taste curries, spices and juicy tropical fruits. Time to listen to happy sounds in an open-air market, a welcoming *meke* (Fijian dance entertainment) or birds in the rainforest. Time to stop and talk and linger and relish; discovering that, in Fiji, time is more than a measurement.

With more than 330 islands, Fiji is also about choice, about deciding what you want and selecting your destination. What activities would you like to do? What's best for families, honeymooners, revellers or intrepid travellers? You need to visit more than a single location to sample the real Fiji.

For city life there's Suva, the nation's capital, with shops, restaurants, markets, a lively nightlife and the seat of government. Cruise and indulge yourself in the Yasawas, or go kayaking in Kadavu. Choose Nananu-i-Ra for windsurfing, kite-surfing and a relaxing lifestyle, or the Mamanuca Group for family fun, world-class surf breaks and island-hopping. Taveuni has rainforests and reefs. Levuka, on Ovalau, retains reminders of the colonial era. Sail to the remote Lau Group – halfway to Tonga – to experience the blending of Fijian and Tongan cultures. Or be pampered and indulge yourself on an exclusive island resort.

Totoya Island, part of the Lau Group

When you've selected a place, consider the pace. In Fiji you can do everything or nothing. Those with a sense of adventure should venture inland on the larger islands, experiencing a rugged interior with rivers, rainforests, waterfalls and wildlife. The unspoilt northern islands embody an unhurried, traditional Fijian way of life. Here lovers of nature are enticed with sightings of exotic birds, or snorkel or dive on rainbow-coloured reefs.

On Viti Levu, visitors can hire a car or take a tour along the Sunshine Coast, which stretches from the sugar capital of Lautoka to Rakiraki on the island's northernmost tip, or head west-southwest along the beautiful Coral Coast, past cane fields and beachfront resorts and on to Pacific Harbour, with its marina, resorts, shops and Arts Village.

VITI LEVU – AROUND NADI

Nadi

Tucked snugly between ocean and mountains is **Nadi**, Fiji's third-largest urban area. From a small community of cane farmers and shopkeepers, Nadi has grown to become a vibrant and bustling Pacific town of around 25,000 inhabitants, and is undisputedly Fiji's tourism capital. Most visitors to Fiji arrive at Nadi International Airport, which is 9km (5½ miles) from the town and within easy reach of the country's main concentration of hotels and resorts. Denarau Marina, located about 20 minutes away, is the departure point for the Yasawa and Mamanuca islands. Other destinations within Fiji can be reached by domestic flight from the airport.

Nadi is, to a large extent, a place of transit for visitors heading to resorts elsewhere. The city itself is basically a long main street lined with shops selling clothes, souvenirs and electronic goods. Shopkeepers try to entice travellers to come inside for 'best deals' and 'unique' items. Sales assistants are masters of selling techniques, and shoppers may be lucky to come away without buying something.

Nadi has a large Indian population, and is a religious centre for both Muslims and Hindus. Spectacularly colourful, the **Sri Siva Subramaniya Swami Temple** on the east side of town is said to be the largest Hindu temple in the southern hemisphere. Visitors are welcomed, but there are certain protocols to be observed. You must remove your shoes and move quietly and respectfully around the confines, and cameras are forbidden on the temple grounds. There is an atmosphere of devout peacefulness as sari-clad women rustle past with small offerings for the various shrines. Tickets for a temple tour can be purchased from the manager's office.

Near Nadi are several brown, sandy and not very attractive beaches. **Nadi Bay Beach** is considered the main one. It's a tidal beach with the sandy area becoming reasonably

Sri Siva Subramaniya Swami Temple

Exotic species abound in the Garden of the Sleeping Giant

wide at low tide. It's good for swimming, but the lack of a reef makes it a bland snorkelling location. However, its west-facing aspect makes it ideal for watching sunsets, which are truly spectacular. Nearby **Wailoaloa Beach** has a number of backpacker establishments. For a more appealing beach scene, head to Denarau *(see page 30)*, with its beach of imported white sand, or take a trip to the offshore islands *(see page 30)*.

North of Nadi

From Nadi, you can join a scheduled tour or travel independently into the Nausori Highlands, a dramatic mountainous region very different in character to the hot, dry, dusty town. A major attraction is the **Garden of the Sleeping Giant** (open Mon–Sat 9am–5pm and Sun mornings; admission fee), located in a shady valley in the foothills of the **Sabeto Range**, an easy 10-minute drive north of Nadi. This attractive, landscaped garden was established by the American actor Raymond Burr in 1977 to house his specialised collection of orchids. The garden now has thousands of orchid and other plant species. A walk of about 45 minutes leads along a boardwalk through the gardens, past orchids, lily ponds and native rainforest.

Take a bus or drive to **Viseisei Village**, 9.5km (6 miles) north of Nadi Airport. Said to be the oldest settlement in Fiji, it was occupied by the people who arrived at nearby **Vuda Point** in great ocean-going canoes around 1500BC. If you are driving, the picturesque tree-lined road is sealed, but watch for speed bumps and pedestrians. You can join an organised tour of the village, but independent travellers are welcome, too. Don't forget to offer village guides payment for their services. The money goes directly to maintaining the village.

Viseisei is not a traditional village of thatched-roof *bures*, but has small, basic and neatly maintained wooden buildings. In the middle of the village is the John Wesley Methodist Church. Outside, facing the *bure* of the chief or Tui Vuda, is a monument commemorating the arrival of the missionaries. Local women sell their crafts from stalls on the village green, so this is a good place to buy genuine souvenirs. Visitors are welcome to attend Sunday church services at 10am and 5pm.

One of the newest developments in this area is the circular-shaped **Vuda Point Marina**, which has a chandlery, fuel dock, coffee shop, Internet access and grocery store.

Choir practice in Viseisei church

Luxury yachts at Denarau Marina

Denarau

Denarau Island is an upmarket resort area 20 minutes' drive south of the airport and linked to the mainland by a bridge. The island's facilities cater almost exclusively to the needs of tourists – Fijians say that when they cross the bridge to Denarau it is as if they are going to a different country. You won't find traditional Fiji here, but you will find a marina, a white-sand beach and several resorts, including three Sheraton properties and a Sofitel. Many resort guests venture no further than the pool or bar. Others spend time at the Denarau Golf and Racquet Club *(see page 90)*, an 18-hole championship course with restaurant and golf shop.

Denarau Marina is the transport hub for ferries and fast catamarans that transfer tourists to and from the **Mamanuca** and **Yasawa islands**. It's also a port for visiting yachts and the departure point for jet-boats that take thrill-seekers through the winding waterways of the Nadi River.

NADI OFFSHORE ISLANDS

The Mamanucas

Synonymous with fun and freedom, the **Mamanuca Group** (pronounced 'mamanu-tha'), west of Nadi, are playful, party islands ideally suited for families and frolickers. Fourteen small islands in the group host 25 tourist resorts. Daily ferries, small aircraft, helicopters and seaplanes ply the air and water, transferring tourists from Nadi, a 10-minute flight or one-hour boat ride away.

With their endless sunshine, beaches of fine white sand and fringing coral reefs, the Mamanucas were some of the first islands in Fiji to be developed for tourism. Geologically, they are a mixture: some are of volcanic origin (**Malolo**, **Mana**, **Tokoriki**), while others are tiny coral cays (**Beachcomber**, **Treasure**, **Navini**). They offer the opportunity to swim, snorkel, dive, sunbathe, fish, kayak, parasail, water-ski or go coral viewing. Evening entertainment includes *lovo* and *meke*, and, for most people staying on the islands, these events are probably the closest they'll get to sampling Fijian culture.

The westernmost islands in the group allow access to some remote and spectacular coral reefs. The diving is good year-round, with sunny, dry weather, good visibility and excellent dive options for novices. Among the top dive sites is The Supermarket, where divers can feed the resident reef sharks.

Up, up and away!

The reefs of the southern Mamanucas are famous for their surf breaks: Wilkes, Namotu Left and Cloud-break. **Tavarua** and **Namotu** islands cater especially for surfers.

Once on an island, visitors are by no means stranded. Sailing trips and daily excursions, organised through your resort, mean that you can visit unpoilt beaches for a barbecue or socialise with other holidaymakers.

On most islands, there's a choice of accommodation, from basic backpacker to upscale resorts, all with their own restaurants and meal plans.

Plantation Island, which is actually part of **Malololailai**, has a nine-hole golf course. In **Musket Cove Resort**, also on Malololailai, is the region's main marina, which offers refuelling, shopping and services. A week-long regatta is held at Musket Cove every September.

The Yasawas

To north of the Mamanucas is the **Yasawa Group** (pronounced 'yah-sow-wah'), a scattering of six large and 14 smaller islands within 135 sq km (52 sq miles) of ocean, stretching approximately 80km (50 miles) from north to south. They are home to some 5,000 people. The Yasawas are what island dreams are made of: crystal-clear blue lagoons, tropical sunshine, isolated white-sand beaches and dramatic volcanic rock outcrops. Beyond these natural attributes, what makes these islands so special is the feeling of remoteness they engender in visitors. In fact, daily fast catamaran ferries from Denarau and seaplane flights from Nadi mean that they are probably more accessible than many of Fiji's other islands.

Healthy coral reefs surrounding most of the islands entice visiting divers. Hikes up, over and around many of the main islands reward walkers with great views

> Part of the Yasawa Group, Nanuya Levu (Turtle Island) first gained recognition as the location of the 1949 and 1980 *Blue Lagoon* films. The filmmakers used the island's natural assets to portray a South Pacific paradise. That image continues to lure visitors to the island's luxury resort, which in 2006 was named world's number-one eco-lodge by *Outside* magazine.

Snorkelling in the Blue Lagoon

and a sense of treading on virgin territory. Many of the islands have dome-shaped hills, some with summits close to 600m (2,000ft) above sea level.

The **Yasawa Flyer** (<www.awesomefiji.com>) sails daily from Denarau Marina (Nadi) to Nacula Island, stopping at any resort as required (the trip takes two to five hours, depending on the location of the destination island). A seven-day Bula Pass enables you to hop from one island to another.

There are no phones, banks, medical or postal facilities on the islands, but your resort can generally help with most needs. Island accommodation is aimed mainly at backpacker and the more upmarket 'flashpacker' tourist, but there are a small number of luxury resorts. For information on some of the resorts on Nacula, Tavewa, Nanuya Lailai and Mata-cawalevu islands, visit <www.fijibudget.com>. **Nanuya Levu** (Turtle Island) is home to one of the world's most famous and exclusive eco-lodges, Turtle Island Resort. If your bank balance can take the strain, spend a minimum of six days luxuriating in this idyllic setting, the height of indulgence for celebrities, romantics and the merely rich.

Yasawa Island, the northernmost member of the group, is famous for its gorgeous beaches, which include Paradise Beach, Champagne Beach, Atus Beach, Lovers Beach and Valawalu Beach. One of the resorts here, Yasawa Beach Resort, fronts a lovely 1km (⅗-mile) stretch of sand.

Off the southern tip of Yasawa Island is the distinctive rocky outcrop of **Sawa-i-Lau**. Inside this limestone monolith is a huge, dome-shaped cave with a natural pool. Unexplained paintings and inscriptions can be seen on the inner chamber walls. Tours to the island are offered by most Yasawa resorts.

Naviti, the largest of the Yasawa Group, has a variety of interesting walks, one of which traverses the backbone of the island and offers extensive coastal views across the Yasawas.

The view to Waya Island at dusk

It makes sense to walk in the early morning or late evening as there are no trees or shade from the sun. It's possible for the fit and hardy to walk the entire length of the island following local tracks that link small fishing villages.

Off the southern tip of Naviti, between the small islands of Nanuya Balavu and Drawaqa, is a warm, shallow lagoon. From May to October each year, squadrons of manta rays feed in these nutrient-rich waters. Divers and snorkellers have the opportunity to witness the impressive nautical acrobatics of these creatures, which soar through the waters, scooping plankton into their mouths with their paddle-like fins. From November, the rays head for deeper waters. Diving throughout the Yasawas is uncrowded and memorable. Several companies offer full professional scuba-diving trips, as well as snorkelling opportunities.

Reef surfing is also possible off the western tip of Nanuya Balavu between November and April. Surfers must bring their own boards.

Waya Island, situated in the southern part of the Yasawas, is one of the most beautiful islands in the group. Walking tracks with great views run along the island's coast. Waya is a two-hour ride from Nadi aboard the Yasawa Flyer or the Waya Lailai resort boat, which departs from Lautoka, north of Nadi on Viti Levu.

Cruise ships departing from Lautoka offer a comfortable way to explore the islands, and have the advantage of being able to change anchorages and routes according to the weather. Plenty of opportunities for onshore cultural excursions are included. **Blue Lagoon Cruises** (<www.bluelagoon cruises.com>) pioneered cruises in the Yasawa Group and is still among the best operators.

If you prefer something more physically demanding than a cruise, you can kayak the islands on a nine-day safari with **Southern Sea Ventures** (<www.southernseaventures.com>).

Volcanic **Rotuma**, lying 450km (720 miles) northwest of Viti Levu, is the most isolated of all Fiji's islands. It is counted as part of the Yasawa Group mainly for political and administrative reasons. This small island's colourful past includes invading Tongans, runaway sailors and soul-saving missionaries. Rotuma does not actively encourage tourism, but for those intent on visiting this outpost, a two-hour Air Fiji flight and a Rotuman contact for accommodation will give you access to one of Fiji's lesser-known destinations.

VITI LEVU'S SUNSHINE COAST/KINGS RD

Viti Levu's **Sunshine Coast**, named for its high count of sunshine hours, stretches along the Kings Road from the sugar capital of Lautoka to Rakiraki on the northwestern coast of Viti Levu, a two-and-a-half-hour drive without stops. Although the roads are poor and the area lacks facilities for tourists, the journey is worth taking for the coastal views and the region's unspoilt natural beauty. Along the way, masses of mangroves line the coast, and fishermen sell strings of reef fish and crabs from roadside stalls. Hiring a car is the best way to see this region, as there are few tours. You'll need a four-wheel-drive vehicle if you want to visit Navala (see page 39).

The Story of Sugar Cane

A Fijian myth explains humanity's orgins. Two Melanesian fishermen, To-Kabwana and To-Karavuvu, found a piece of sugar cane in their net one day. They threw it back into the sea, but after catching it again, decided to keep it. They painted the stalk a bright colour and left it as decoration. Then an unexpected thing happened. The cane burst open, and a woman came out. She cooked food for the men, but hid herself at night. Finally she was captured and became the wife of one of the men. From their union sprang the whole human race.

Lautoka and Around

Lautoka, 33km (53 miles) north of Nadi, is Fiji's second-largest city, with a population of 80,000. Pieces of sugar cane lying on the roads leading into town leave no doubt as to the main industry here. This is Fiji's sugar capital, home to the nation's largest sugar mill. As well as the sugar industry, the city's economy is sustained by the production of soaps, oils, timber, steel and garments.

The shopping centre is centrally located along **Vitogo Parade**, which has a picturesque row of royal palms running parallel to the narrow-gauge railway track

Railway tracks, Lautoka

that's used to transport sugar cane. Not really a tourist town, Lautoka does nevertheless have a certain sophistication lacking in other commercial centres. The **municipal markets** have a bustling, multicultural ambience, with Indian, Fijian and Chinese stallholders selling fresh fruit and vegetables. Elsewhere, the **Girmit Centre**, an Indian cultural centre, caters to the city's large Indian population.

When visiting Lautoka, watch out for street con artists who to try to inveigle tourists into giving them money by brandishing letters asking for support for a relative with a medical condition. Just ignore them, although they can be hard to shake off.

Ten kilometres (6 miles) southeast of Lautoka is the **Koroyanitu National Heritage Park**, in the Nausori Highlands.

Six villages within the park work together as part of an eco-tourism venture. Tracks wind through native forests and grasslands. Information about the park and village accommodation can be found at the Abaca Visitors' Centre (tel: 666 6644 and dial 1234 after the beep; admission fee).

Ba to Rakiraki

Further east from Lautoka, a short detour off the Kings Road leads to the town of **Ba**. There's not a great deal to see here, but Ba makes a good place to stay overnight for those wanting to take their time touring the area. The sculpture of an eagle and globe held in a huge pair of hands, in the central roundabout leading into town, was created to commemorate the new millennium.

From Ba, a one-and-a-half-hour drive inland to the southeast along a dusty, narrow and winding road brings you to the

Living the traditional life in Navala

➤ village of **Navala** in the Nausori Highlands. A four-wheel-drive vehicle is recommended for this trip (and only in the dry season, May to November), or you can take a bus from Ba; the only other option is to take a tour from Lautoka or Nadi.

Navala is home to about 800 people, all of whom live in traditional thatched *bures*. Visitors are expected to bring a *sevusevu* (gift) of *yaqona* (kava) for the chief of the village and to take part in the kava ceremony *(see page 105)*. If you are travelling independently, chances are that before you enter the village you will be greeted by villagers vying for the opportunity to act as guides; expect to pay a guide fee.

Back on the Kings Road, heading east, is **Tavua**, a market town with a relaxed atmosphere. It's a good place to stock up on food and fresh fruit. Continuing eastwards, you pass through magnificent scenery as the road makes its way down from the mountains and into the **Rakiraki region**. This stretch of coast, the northernmost of Viti Levu, combines the lush tropical climate of the east with the sunny, drier climate of the west. The sunrises and sunsets here are particularly stunning.

About 10km (6 miles) before the village of Rakiraki, you can't help but notice the large outcrop of **Navatu Rock**. There is only one access route to the top, a factor that made it a secure site for a village during earlier, more hostile times. If you look carefully from the highway, you will see a small island about 1–1.5km (1 mile) from the coast, rising to about 180m (594ft) above the sea. Fijian legend deems this as the departure point for disembodied spirits journeying into the afterlife.

On the south side of the road leading into Rakiraki, just before a triangular intersection, is **Ratu Udre Udre's tomb**. This cannibal chief kept a stone tally of over 800 people he consumed before his own death in the mid-1800s.

Rakiraki itself is a small, unremarkable agricultural settlement. It's a good place to buy food before heading to self-catering accommodation on the island of Nananu-i-Ra.

Sunset on Nananu-i-Ra

About 7km (4 miles) to the east of Rakiraki is the turn-off to **Ellington Wharf**. From here, ferries and water taxis depart for Nananu-i-Ra and the outer islands. **Nananu-i-Ra**, 5km (3 miles) off the northern Viti Levu coast, is popular with visitors who want a laid-back holiday in a natural setting without travelling too far from Nadi.

The island's name means 'dreamland of the west'. A local legend tells of a young chief from Vanua Levu falling in love with a beautiful villager from from Viti Levu. The relationship was frowned upon by elders, so the star-crossed lovers escaped to Nananu-i-Ra to be together in their dreamland.

For many years the island has been the location of small backpacker-style accommodation, but more expansive development is under way. The white-sand beaches are pretty, and the snorkelling directly off the island is good. Scuba-diving sites nearby are some of Fiji's best. If you're into walking, a hike around the island will take less than four hours.

Eastern Viti Levu

On a hill near the village of **Naiserelagi**, 45km (28 miles) east of Rakiraki on the Kings Road, is a large, concrete church. Inside is a beautiful mural of the Black Christ wearing a *masi (tapa)* loincloth, painted by French artist Jean Charlot in 1962. The church is easy to miss, so watch out for the village of Nanukuloa; Naiserelagi is the next village to the south. Once there, keep an eye out for the Ra Maternity Clinic, and then take an uphill right towards the Navunibitu Catholic Mission. The church is behind St Francis Xavier School.

Despite the area's stunning scenery, tourists rarely go much further eastwards than here, deterred by the state of the road. A potholed gravel track winds for more than 100km (60 miles) to Korovou, where the tarmac road begins again. Small, tidy villages appear every so often, but none appear to have shops, petrol or toilets. Be prepared to smile, stop and talk to all you meet. The locals don't get many visitors and love the opportunity to shake hands and chat.

As you near **Korovou** the landscape changes from forest to dairyland. Dairying was established here by British ex-soldiers at the end of World War I after local Fijian chiefs gave them the land. Prior to independence in 1970, some farmers began selling their land to the highest bidders, in most cases Indians. This angered the chiefs, who maintained that if the farmers did not want the land any more, they should give it back to the villagers. A system has since been established to give former local landowners first chance to buy farms put up for sale.

Mural of the Black Christ

Coral Coast Railway

VITI LEVU'S CORAL COAST/QUEENS RD

The Queens Road is the highway leading from Lautoka to Suva along the southern coast of Viti Levu. The stretch between Momi and Pacific Harbour (about two hours' drive without stops) is known as the Coral Coast because of the large platform reef formations that lie directly offshore. A number of luxury resorts pepper the shoreline with easy access to safe swimming and snorkelling at high tide. At low tide, it is possible to wade through ankle-deep water to the reef edge, where ocean meets lagoon.

➤ The **Coral Coast** is arguably the most spectacular scenic drive in Fiji. The road winds beside the coastline, where calm and crystal-clear water covers shallow reefs and frills their edges in a wash of white, and then cuts back through rounded bush-clad hills before re-emerging on the coast. Along the way there are sugar-cane fields, villages and, of course, beaches.

Admittedly, the Coral Coast beaches are not Fiji's best. With the exception of Natadola Beach, they tend to be rocky and covered in dead coral. But at high tide, when the shallow reef is covered with water, the colours and reflections are beautiful.

Nadi to Sigatoka

The turn-off for **Momi Guns** (open daily 9am–5pm; admission fee), a World War II battery, is 18km (29 miles) south of Nadi on the Queens Road. Inside an old bunker is a small museum whose walls are covered in historic photos showing Fijian soldiers in World War II uniforms. Other photos illustrate the restoration of the Momi Guns site. Momi was a key strategic link between the US and Australia during World War II when Japanese forces were active in the Pacific. However, the only time the guns were fired was at a New Zealand vessel that had not clearly identified itself.

A short distance before the town of Sigatoka, at Cuvu, is the western end of the **Coral Coast Railway** (tel: 652 8731; train departs from the causeway to the Shangri-La Fijian Resort at 10am and returns at 4pm daily; fee includes lunch). A No. 11 steam train hauled sugar cane along the trail from 1940 to 1960, when it was replaced by diesel locomotives. Now lovingly restored, it transports tourists on a scenic coastal ride that ends at **Natadola Beach**.

This white-sand beach is a great place to laze in the sun. The swimming and body-surfing are good too, but there can sometimes be a strong undercurrent, so care should be taken. This beautiful spot, once remote from development, has come under increasing pressure from developers, and a number of resorts are now under construction along the shoreline.

Sigatoka and Surrounds

About 69km (43 miles) from Nadi is **Sigatoka** (pronounced 'sing-a-toka'), sited at the mouth of the wide, brown, snaking

Sigatoka River. Around 8,000 people live here. Tourist facilities sit comfortably within a small-town atmosphere, and it's easy to go about your business without being drawn into obvious tourist traps. Locals stream unhurriedly across the long bridge that stretches across the river. Abandoned *bilibilis* can be seen washed up along the shoreline. These disposable bamboo rafts are used to bring goods and produce down the river, and are affectionately referred to by some locals as 'HMS No-Come-Back'. Proceeds from the sale of market goods are used to buy a bus ticket back to the villages; a new *bilibili* will be constructed for the next trip into town.

About 2km (1¼ miles) south of the town, near Kulukulu Village, are the **Sigatoka Sand Dunes** (open daily 9am–4.30pm; admission fee). The area is both a national park, approximately 5km (3 miles) long and 1km (⅔ mile) wide, and an important archaeological site, where shards of pottery and

Sigatoka Sand Dunes

skeletal remains are periodically uncovered by the wind. Carbon dating estimates the remains range from between 5BC and AD240. The undulating dunes hug the coastline for several kilometres; those furthest from the sea are covered in vegetation. Some dunes are 30–45m (100–150ft) high, and there are wonderful views from their summits. The information centre, which is run by volunteers, has some excellent illustrations and displays. Take care when walking on the dunes: the sand is extremely hot. Wear well-fitting shoes; the soles of your feet will burn in anything less. It's a good idea to bring water, too, and, of course, swimwear.

The Melanesian style of pottery is still practised in the small villages of the Sigatoka Valley, where the women dig and shape clay into coil or slab pots. Neat rows of pots dry in the sun before they are heated over an open fire. While each pot is hot, resin from *dakua* (kauri) gum is rubbed on the exterior to create a varnish that brings out the colour of the clay and makes the pot watertight.

High on a bluff overlooking the Sigatoka River, 4km (2½ miles) inland, to the east of Sigatoka, are the remains of a fortified village. The **Tavuni Hill Fort** (open Mon–Fri 8am–5pm, Sat 8.30am–1.30pm; admission fee) is a national archaeological site, and the abandoned ruins have been cleared and excavated for easy viewing. Among the items on display in the site's small museum is an underground oven in which human bones were found. A guide is available who will point out many features which would otherwise go unnoticed.

The **Sigatoka Valley**, divided by the river into two main agricultural areas, is rich and fertile. Half of the valley is used for growing taro, cassava and other fruit and vegetable crops. The eastern side of the valley is kept for sugar cane.

Sigatoka marks the end of the cane-growing region, as from here on the rainfall is greater (sugar cane needs a dry season to grow properly).

The Sigatoka Valley is one of the few areas remaining where Fijian pottery is still made in the traditional manner. The agile women of **Nakabuta Village**, about 3km (2 miles) from Sigatoka, sit cross-legged on the dirt floor of their huts and gently massage lumps of local clay into pots and other pieces which are then glazed with tree gum and fired.

Heading east on the Queens Road again, you soon pass through the village of Korotogo before making a short detour to **Kula Eco Park**, nestled in coastal forest. This is Fiji's only wildlife park. Here you'll see many of the islands' native species, including fruit bats, parrots, falcons, goshawks and the endangered Fijian crested iguana. Hawksbill sea turtles are hand-fed daily. Wooden walkways, winding paths and swinging bridges lead over and around a cooling stream. Provided you don't visit at the same time as a school group taking advantage of the educational facilities, you'll be able to enjoy the diverse sounds of the bush dwellers.

Back on the Queens Road, from here on the scenery slowly changes from rolling hills to rainforest, an indication that you are heading into the wet, tropical side of Viti Levu. Small fishing villages shaded by rainforest vegetation are scattered along the highway, showing just how close these two worlds are on this section of coast.

Pacific Harbour

Pacific Harbour is located at the eastern end of the Coral Coast, 50km (31 miles) west of Suva. It's an upmarket canal development dotted with flash expatriate housing and the brightly coloured, hard-to-miss Arts Village. This is an area ideally suited to visitors who like some outdoor action, with superb diving and fishing offshore in the Beqa Lagoon, a world-class surf break at Yanuca Island and, inland, wild rivers to raft. Here also is the famous **Greens South Pacific Golf Course** (tel: 345 0022 for details and rental fee), designed by Robert Trent Jones Jr, for those dedicated enough to want to play golf in the tropical heat.

➤ The **Arts Village** (open Mon–Sat 9am–4pm; admission fee; <www.artsvillage.com>) comprises two distinct aspects. The commercial complex has more than 60 businesses, including banks, boutiques, assorted eateries and an Internet café; the village's cultural ventures give visitors a crash course in Fijian culture.

Putting on a show at the Pacific Harbour Arts Village

You will need a full day to enjoy the village. Cultural shows begin with an energetic, entertaining and mesmerising display of firewalking, dance and drama, performed by people from nearby Beqa Island *(see page 48)*. Then visitors board twin-hulled canoes, which are poled around a river lagoon. The canoes stop close to a number of *bures* by the shore, each depicting a different aspect of traditional Fijian village life: the making of *masi (tapa),* fishing, carving, pottery and cooking. The final part of the excursion involves a thought-provoking visit to the temple of the chief, where you are presented with a fascinating insight into the spiritual basis of the traditional Fijian way of life.

Rafting the Navua River

Pacific Harbour is the departure point for trips to the **Upper Navua River**, which slices a deep chasm through Viti Levu's interior about one-and-a-half hour's drive north of the town. From its base in Pacific Harbour, Rivers Fiji (tel: 345 0147; <www.riversfiji.com>) offers guided excursions on the river, using white-water rafts and inflatable kayaks to negotiate rapids and penetrate canyons and vegetation-shrouded waterways. The company also leads day trips on the **Luva River**, which flows into the Navua. This tour is a good way to see the mountainous scenery of the **Namosi Highlands**. As well as a paddle on the river, the Luva tour includes a hike up to the **Wainutu Falls** and a kava ceremony with local villagers.

Coral Coast Islands

There are a number of islands off the Coral Coast. Unlike in the Mamanucas and Yasawas, there is no regular ferry service linking them with the mainland. If you are staying on one these islands, transport is organised by your resort.

Beqa Island (pronounced 'benga') is visible from Pacific Harbour, lying 7.5km (5 miles) offshore. The roughly circular island, about 7km (4½ miles) in diameter, has a rugged interior, but it's the 64km (40-mile) long coral reef surrounding Beqa that attracts most visitors. The reef provides good conditions for diving and snorkelling. Specialist dive operators on Beqa (and Vatulele, *see below*) organise dive trips around Beqa Lagoon and the surrounding reefs. Among the best dive sites are Side Streets, Caesar's Rocks and Frigate Pass.

Inside Beqa Lagoon and 9km (6 miles) west of Beqa Island is tiny **Yanuca Island**, whose proximity to the world-class surf breaks at Frigate Passage makes it a surfer's mecca. There are two surf camps and one small village.

Well to the west of Beqa Lagoon, 32km (20 miles) off Korolevu, is the beautiful and romantic island of **Vatulele** (pronounced 'vah-too-lay-lay'). Shaped like a footprint, Vatulele is about 13km (8 miles) in length. It is low-lying, with its highest point only 33m (108ft) above sea level. The island's northern and eastern coasts are protected by a barrier

Firewalking

Demonstrations of firewalking are commonly staged at larger hotels and at the Pacific Harbour Arts Village. An enormous bonfire is first built under a pile of stones. When the stones glow red, they are raked. Now the participants appear in ceremonial dress, and with deep, resonating chants, walk slowly across the stones – stopping to wave and smile at the crowds – in what appears to be complete immunity to pain. You can really feel the heat. At one ceremony on Beqa, a scientist measured the temperature of the stones at over 650°C (120°F).

These performances are aimed at entertaining tourists, but the practice began as a solemn rite for special occasions. According to legend, the ability to walk barefoot on hot stones without injury was granted by Veli, the leader of a group of petty gods, to Tui Qalita, a chief on the island of Beqa. The descendants of Tui Qalita now act as instructors in the art.

reef that ranges up to 2km (1¼ miles) from the shoreline. The white-sand beaches are stunning. Almost totally composed of limestone, the island has a number of caves and pools.

About two-thirds of the island is covered by thick vegetation, which has not been affected by any major human activity. In fact, apart from the single resort, there has been no 'Western' development on the island. Some 900 Fijians live in the island's four villages, which are Fiji's main producers of *masi (tapa)*. The method of making this bark cloth is laborious. It involves stripping the bark from a certain type of mulberry tree, soaking it in water, scraping it with shells and pounded it into thin sheets, which are then layered, pounded together and painted.

In general, the only visitors to experience this magical place are guests at the upmarket Vatulele Island Resort or tourists on charter-boat excursions. Transfers to the island are by resort charter plane.

Suva

At the southeastern corner of Viti Levu is steamy **Suva**, a harbour city sited on a hilly peninsula between Laucala Bay and Suva Harbour. Home of the government, the University of the South Pacific and the Fiji School of Medicine, Suva is the political, educational and business centre of Fiji.

Except on Sunday, when the city lies idle, Suva is a buzzing, multicultural South Pacific medley of a place, with a diverse populaton of mainly Fijians, Indians, other Pacific Islanders and Chinese. About 200,000 people live here, and another 60,000 live along the 25km (16-mile) stretch between the city and the airport at Nausori, 30 minutes to the northeast. Markets, food, restaurants and shops reflect Suva's ethnic diversity.

If you don't mind the heat and are relatively fit, Suva's main sights are mostly within easy walking distance of one

Government Buildings at Suva

another, and can be seen in a single day. Start from the centre with the section of **Victoria Parade** that stretches from the post office to Thurston Gardens. Just opposite the post office, in a small, tree-shaded building that stands out amid the large surrounding commercial structures, is the Fiji Visitors' Bureau office, where you can find information on the city and islands. Along Victoria Parade are many historic buildings, including the Victorian-era **Old Town Hall**, in its time the epicentre of the performing arts. Next to it is the **Suva City Library**, built in 1909 with funds donated by Scottish-American steel magnate and philanthropist Andrew Carnegie.

Heading south along the parade, statues of Ratu Cakobau and Ratu Sukuna silently watch over the grey, forbidding old **Government Buildings** on the left (the new Parliament Building on Ratu Sukuna Road opened in 1992). A short distance further on is **Albert Park**, part of a grant of land to the colonial government from the Australia-based Polynesia

Clock tower in Thurston Gardens

Company as an inducement to move the capital from Levuka to Suva (the move officially took place in 1882). The park is well used, with a cricket pitch and tennis courts. In 1928, Australian aviator Charles Kingsford Smith landed his plane *The Southern Cross* in the park, one of two stopovers on the first trans-Pacific flight from the US to Australia.

On the opposite side of Victoria Parade is the **Grand Pacific Hotel**, dating from 1914, which in its heyday set the standard for luxury accommodation in the South Pacific. Now closed, it has been undergoing a lengthy renovation. The stately palms which now line the front of the Grand Pacific Hotel were planted to replace those that had to be cut down so that Kingsford Smith could land his plane.

Next to Albert Park are **Thurston Gardens**, which opened in 1913. Within the gardens is the **Fiji Museum** (open Mon–Fri 8.30am–4.30pm, Sat 9am–4.30pm, Sun 1pm–4pm; admission fee; <www.fijimuseam.org.fj>). This research and educational institute, founded in 1904, houses the world's most comprehensive collection of Fijian artefacts. Among them are grisly reminders of Fiji's cannibal past, pottery, archaeological finds, relics from the *Bounty,* and a replica of a huge *drua* – a double-hulled sailing canoe.

Back near the beginning of Victoria Parade is **The Tri-angle**, a smaller park with plenty of seats on which to sit and watch the world go by. In the centre of the park is a historical marker with four inscriptions. There's nothing particularly exciting about that, except that three of them are wrong. 'Suva Proclaimed Capital in 1882.' Not so. The home government approved the move from Levuka to Suva in 1877, but it wasn't made official until 1882. 'Cross and Cargill First Missionaries arrived 14th October 1835.' According to their diaries, it was the 12th. 'Public Land Sales on this spot 1880.' Sales actually took place further down the road. 'British Crown Colony 10th October 1874.' Finally, something they got right.

Nearby, on Pratt Street, is the **Roman Catholic Cathedral**, built in 1902. With its two towers, it's one of the city's most prominent landmarks.

Suva is as good a place as any to pick up a bargain in Fiji. Made-to-measure clothing is inexpensive and can be put together by a tailor in record time. For more shopping opportunities, try the **Handicraft Market**, near the waterfront on the ground level of a large parking garage directly behind the Westpac Bank building. Here you'll find mats, baskets, bowls and other crafts from throughout the islands. The Flea Market on Rodwell Street has a real, untouristy local flavour. A stroll away from the Flea Market is the lively **Municipal Market**, where stallholders display colourful

Twenty minutes' drive west of Suva along the Queens Road is the Wainadoi Spice Gardens, a 9-hectare (22-acre) property where spices are grown organically. This is the base for a network of small village farmers who grow nutmeg, cardamom, ginger, vanilla and peppercorns for both the domestic and export markets.

mounds of fruit and vegetables, spices, strings of reef fish and all manner of other goods for sale. The market is open every day of the week except Sunday.

Around Suva

If Suva's humidity gets you down, retreat to the shade of **Colo-i-Suva Forest Park** (open daily 8am–4pm; admission fee), 11km (7 miles) north of the capital, where you'll find walking trails, rainforest, flowing water and birdsong. If you take your walking seriously and like to combine it with climbing, set out for Joske's Thumb, a tall volcanic peak. (Before climbing, check with the Fiji Visitors' Bureau in Suva that climbing conditions are suitable and that access is permitted.)

About 20km (12 miles) northeast of Suva is the town of **Nausori**, the site of Fiji's second international airport. Water taxis can be hired to explore the delta of the Rewa River.

Colo-i-Suva

Nausori is the departure point for boats to **Bau**, a tiny island just off the coast that was once Fiji's seat of power *(see page 16)*. You can't just go there at will. You must have permission from a Bau islander who will escort you around, or from the Ministry of Fijian Affairs. Bau has the oldest church in the country, a fascinating cemetery, and a large stone once used to crush human skulls.

> **When in 1854 Ratu Cakobau was converted to Christianity, he ordered the destruction of the old pagan temple on Bau where human sacrifices were carried out. The stones were moved to the other end of the village where they were used to construct a church. The head bashing stone became the church baptismal font.**

LOMAIVITI GROUP

The Lomaiviti Group of islands lies off the east coast of Viti Levu. Ovalau, Leleuvia, Caqalai and Yanuca Lailai are the major islands.

Ovalau

Catching a ride on the daily ferry service from Suva or a 10-minute flight from Nausori Airport will get you to **Ovalau** (pronounced 'o-vah-lau'), the principal island of the Lomaiviti Group, with a history and energy all its own. The island is 13km (8 miles) long and 11km (7 miles) across. The main town is **Levuka** (population 1,500), which nestles at the base of a 600m (1,980ft) bluff, on one of the few flat areas on the island. Levuka was Fiji's earliest European settlement and the country's first capital.

The town has a peaceful ambience that is in sharp contrast to its boisterous past. Levuka was once a safe haven for sailors jumping ship, escaped convicts and other assorted misfits. Sandalwood traders stopped here to revictual, build schooners, trade for bêche-de-mer or settle down with Fijian women. For its part, the indigenous population saw the settlers as intruders, and frequently set fire to the town.

By the 1850s, Levuka had a reputation as a place of drunkenness and violence. In the 1870s, planters and settlers arrived, swelling the population to 3,000. In 1874, when Fiji was ceded to the crown, Levuku became the capital of the new British colony. A lack of space to expand created problems, and in 1882 the government moved to Suva, taking most trade with it. Levuka sank into commercial insignificance.

There's plenty to see in Levuka, and the best place to start is the **Levuka Community Centre and Museum** near Queen's Wharf. Originally a storehouse built in 1878, it has been revamped and houses the public library, craft centre, squash court and meeting hall. The centre also offers guided one-and-a-half to two-hour walks of the town for a small fee.

The entrance to **Queen's Wharf** is also home to the post office, Customs office and the Port Authority of Fiji. Opposite the post office is a drinking fountain that was the site of a carrier-pigeon loft which, in the late 1800s, was the Levuka terminal for a pigeon postal service to Suva. The birds covered the 65km (40-mile) distance in about 30 minutes. You can relax and watch activity on the wharf from nearby **Patterson Park**.

A few hundred metres south of here in Nasova is the **Cession Stone**, laid to commemorate the signing of the Deed of Cession between Fiji and Britain. Opposite stands the **Anniversary Bure**, built for Prince Charles to entertain dignitaries when he came to grant Fiji its independence in 1970.

Heading north along **Beach Street** (the main road, but don't expect a beach), you'll probably hear the double chime of the French clock on **Sacred Heart Church**, built by the Marist Fathers in 1858. The light on the spire guides ships through the Levuka Passage. In Levuka's early days, Beach Street was

The Lekuva waterfront at sunset

lined with saloons, but all that remains today are worn-out buildings as faded reminders of a more prosperous era.

On the other side of Totoga Creek is the **Ovalau Club**, Fiji's first gentleman's club, which was once a watering hole for eminent white colonials. Stop off for a drink and ask to see the letter written by the captain of a World War I German sea raider, Count Von Luckner, who was captured on nearby Wakaya Island. Von Luckner abandoned ship when his vessel ran aground elsewhere and landed in a small launch on Katafaga Island in the Lau Group. He broke into a home, took some food, and left payment and a thank-you note signed 'Max Pemberton' (a British writer of adventure stories).

Other sites of interest to the north of here include the 125-year-old **Royal Hotel**, Fiji's oldest hotel – still open for business; the **War Memorial** on Niukaube Hill at the northern end of Beach Street; and on Mission Hill, the Methodist Mission homes and **Holy Redeemer Church**.

The Levuka clock in the tower of the Sacred Heart Roman Catholic Church is possibly the only surviving example of a dual-striking clock still functioning. Its unusual feature is that it repeats the hour and the half hour, striking once and then chiming again a minute later so that townspeople missing the count of the chimes the first time would be able to catch it when it was repeated.

For those with an interest in the more morbid aspects of history, a short distance north of the town in Levuka village is the **Old Methodist Cemetery**, which contains the graves of early settlers, including that of John Brown Williams, the US Consul whose claim for damages helped cause the downfall of Cakobau *(see page 16)*. Further north still, in Cawaci, is the spooky **Bishops' Tomb**, where Fiji's first and second Roman Catholic bishops are buried.

Join a tour or take a taxi to **Silana Village**, 10km (6 miles) from Levuka on the northwest coast of Ovalau. A community project of Aravudi village, Silani allows visitors to experience the old traditions, customs and handicrafts of Fiji.

If you're interested in a walk, join a trekking tour led by Epinera Bole (Epi Tours; tel: 344 0166; email: <lovoni@owlfiji.com>) in the rainforest-clad hills surrounding **Lovoni**, in the centre of the island. Your guide has extensive local knowledge of mythology, traditional medicines, native foods and ecology.

Other Lomaiviti Islands

Other islands in the Lomaiviti Group are worth a visit. **Leleuvia Island**, south of Ovalau in the Moturiki Passage, has white-sand beaches and clear waters. **Caqalai Island** (pronounced 'thung-gulie') is a 5-hectare (14-acre) coral island in the same area, with backpacker accommodation run by the

Methodist Church of Fiji. Both islands are off the main tourist track. From November to February, hawksbill turtles nest on the beaches of Leleuvia and Caqalai islands, as well as Ovalau.

There is good diving in the Lomaiviti Group. Trips leave Levuka daily for Wakaya, Makogai, Vatu, Moturiki and Ovalau reefs. Contact Ovalau Watersports (Ovalau Watersports Centre, Levuka; tel: 344 0166; <www.owlfiji.com>).

KADAVU

With its tropical rainforest, cascading waterfalls, and the mighty splendour of the Great Astrolabe Reef, **Kadavu** (pronounced 'kand-a-vu') has earned for itself a reputation among hikers and divers as one of Fiji's most beautiful islands. One of a remote and rugged group of islands located 100km (60 miles) off Viti Levu's southern coast, Kadavu is Fiji's fourth-largest island, and has a population of around 8,700. The two next largest islands in the Kadavu Group are **Ono** and **Galoa**, and there are many smaller ones. Daily flights to the main town of **Vunisea** operate from both Nadi and Suva airports. There is also a seaplane and a ferry service from Suva.

Kadavu is about 48km (30 miles) in length, and varies in width from 365m (1,200ft) to 13km (8 miles). The coastline

Diving at Kadavu

is craggy and deeply indented – some bays are so indented that they almost split the island. There are rugged, volcanic mountains, the highest being **Nabukelevu (Mount Washington)**, 838m (2,749ft) high. In the isolated villages, the local people still live in the traditional Fijian manner, maintaining their culture and a subsistence lifestyle. Kadavu draws visitors with a love of nature and a desire to do physically challenging activities, whether it be kayaking, surfing, scuba diving or trekking.

Namalata Isthmus, linking the island's western end and its centre, is known to Fijians as Na Yarabale ('the place where the canoes are dragged across'). **Namuana Village**, home of the turtle callers *(see page 62)*, is also in this area.

Kadavu has few roads, and small boats are the island's main form of transport. Each of the island's resorts organises its own boat transfers to and from Vunisea. Trip times can vary from 30 to 60 minutes, depending on the resort's location. Prevailing southeasterly winds batter the exposed southeastern coasts of the Kadavu Group; all of the islands can be subject to inclement weather. Note that many budget resorts use boats with no shelter, which can make for a wet and rough transfer to the more remote locations, especially between April and August.

One of the main attractions of Kadavu is the **Great Astrolabe Reef**, which hooks around the southeastern side of the

island for 45km (28 miles). On its seaward side, this barrier reef drops away to 1,800m (5,940ft). It's a spectacular diving location, with a huge variety of colourful coral, fish and other marine species. Deep walls, reef passages and shallow reef-garden grottoes constitute the diving terrain. The top dive sites include Naingoro Pass, Usbourne Passage, North Astrolabe and Robert's Wreck. The weather has a big impact on diving here, in terms of both accessibility and visibility, which can vary between 15 and 70m (50–230ft), depending on the time of year and conditions.

The indented nature of the coastline makes Kadavu ideal for sea kayaking. The months of May

Sea kayaking, Kadavu

to September offer the most settled weather. For information about sea kayaking at Kadavu, see the Tamarillo Sea Kayaking website, <www.tamarillo.co.nz>. Scuba kayaking – in which divers paddle out to a dive spot by kayak – is also an option in some areas.

Surfing is good here, too. The island's surf resorts offer breaks for beginners and advanced surfers alike. Surf spots include Vesi Passage, off Matava on the south coast, and Cape Washington at the island's westernmost end. Surfing is the main activity for visitors to **Nagigia Island Resort**, which has five breaks just offshore. The resort is located on a tiny island just off Kadavu.

The rainforests that cover Kadavu draw trekkers and birdwatchers. Walks can be organised through most resorts.

The Sacred Turtles of Kadavu

Namuana Village nestles in a bay on Kadavu Island. Here, the women still practise the ancient ritual of turtle calling. According to legend, many years ago in the village of Namuana, the princess Tinaicoboga lived with her daughter Raudalice. The two women often fished around the reefs, but one day waded further out than usual. They were so engrossed in fishing that they failed to notice the approach of a war canoe paddled by warriors from the nearby village of Nabukelevu, who seized the women, bound their hands and feet with vine, and headed for home.

Outraged, the gods of the sea wrought a great storm, and the canoe was swamped with water until it foundered. The warriors saw that the women had changed into turtles, and threw them into the ocean. The storm abated, and they returned to Nabukelevu.

When the women of Namuana sing to them today, descendants of the turtles return to the village. But it is said that if any villagers from Nabukelevu are present the turtles will fail to appear.

View of Savusavu Bay

VANUA LEVU

Although only 64km (40 miles) northeast of Viti Levu, **Vanua Levu** (pronounced 'va-new-ah lay-vu'), the second-largest island of the Fiji archipelago, is less developed and less visited by tourists. Those who do make the trip have opportunities to see local traditions and culture in a relatively unspoilt setting.

The interior of the island is rugged, with sharp mountainous ridges, while the coastline is a winding elongation of irregular indentations surrounded by coral reefs. The island was once a centre for the copra trade, but today it is sugar cultivation that drives the economy. Savusavu is the main tourist centre. A reasonably good road links Savusavu with **Labasa**, just inland from the northern coast. Labasa is a largely Indian community of 25,000 that has thrived and developed thanks to the sugar industry. Essentially a commercial centre, the town is rarely visited by tourists. Hectares of sugar-cane fields flourish on the dry western and northern coasts of the island.

Savusavu

Flanked by a beautiful bay and dramatic mountains covered in darkly green and verdant growth, **Savusavu** (population 5,000) is the focus of tourist interest on Vanua Levu. Originally established as a port for sailing ships plying the coastline for sandalwood and bêche-de-mer (sea cucumber), Savusavu is still the sole port of entry on Vanua Levu and is a popular and lively stopover for yachtsmen and divers.

The main street, 0.5km (⅓ mile) long, is lined with Chinese- and Indian-owned stores with a faded classical elegance. The town has a cared-for feeling, with decorated planter pots complete with tropical palms, and geometrically designed patterns on the concrete lamp posts.

Savusavu Bay

Hot, steaming **springs** bubble up from beneath the earth's crust to the surface, an indication of the geothermal activity simmering beneath the town. Coils of steam swirl from grassy lots and cracks in the pavements, and gushes of boiling water gurgle monotonously in the area adjacent to the Hot Springs Hotel.

In the town, a real-estate frenzy appears to be under way, with Americans, Germans and Australians looking for investment or retirement properties. The bustling economic activity reflects this growth, with an increasing number of restaurants, hotels, resorts and other businesses catering to tourism. Many of the expatriates who have chosen to make Savusavu their home appear to be encouraging eco-friendly development that will be commercially beneficial to the local Fijians.

Central to the harbour activity is **The Copra Shed Marina** (tel: 885 0457; email: <coprashed@connect.com.fj>). The Copra Shed is the town's oldest building

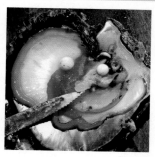

Pearls!

and houses several shops, a restaurant and the **Savusavu Yacht Club**. A new marina complex is being constructed along the town's waterfront that will combine residential and retail facilities. When the project is complete, 130 luxury waterfront villas will spread along 1.5km (1 mile) of the waterfront, changing the face of the town.

A short distance from the western end of the main shopping area are the premises of **J. Hunter Pearls** (open Mon–Fri, tours 9.30am and 1.30pm; tel: 885 0821; <www.pearls fiji.com>; fee for tours). This small, nondescript building houses exquisite and expensive pearl jewellery and is well worth a visit, but take your credit card along – you'll need it. The staff encourage visitors to handle the goods. This is probably the only jewellery shop in the world where a retail assistant will allow a child to hold a black pearl necklace priced at F$22,000. Perhaps they know that what you touch you will want to buy. Take the J. Hunter Pearls tour out into Savusavu Bay to watch oyster farmers go about their work; more than 1 million oysters are seeded, ready for pearls to develop. There's also an opportunity to snorkel among strands of oysters that hang from thousands of multicoloured buoys.

Exploring Vanua Levu

If you like to travel independently, and are prepared to get lost and let things unfold, rather than stick rigidly to a plan, then hire a car, bike or scooter (from Trip n' Tours; tel: 885 3154; email: <tripntours@connect.com.fj>; or from the Copra Shed Marina). Don't expect to find road maps or signs to help you get around. Instead, take time to stop and talk to the villagers. However, if you ask directions from locals be aware that the answer they give you may not actually correspond with the question you asked. But Fijians are extremely obliging and think nothing of accompanying you as a guide, or waving you on your way laden with gifts of pawpaw (papaya) or banana – and they do this with no expectation of payment in return. Alternatively, tours can be arranged through Trip n' Tours, or by negotiating with a taxi driver.

The **Hibiscus Highway** takes in 112km (70 miles) of the coast southeast of Savusavu. Coral reef and mangroves edge the road, and the shallow blue lagoons are punctuated by coral islets sculptured into mushroom shapes by wind and sea.

The stunning reef around Namenalala Island, 25km (15½ miles) off the southeastern coast of Vanua Levu, is protected by a 76 sq km (29 sq mile) marine park in which all commercial fishing is banned. There are 26 dive sites. No reef moorings are allowed, and boats do not drop anchor. Divers are dropped at the dive sites and collected on ascent.

Huge wrought-iron gates just a few kilometres along the highway signal the entrance to Namale Resort, one of the most upmarket resorts in Fiji, and owned by US motivational speaker Tony Robbins. While guests water-ski and jet-ski in the bay, swarms of local Fijian children leap off trees and swim in the nearby river outlet. It's an intoxicating juxtaposition of happiness bought with money, and plain old fun for free.

Beach on Vanua Levu

Also on the Hibiscus Highway is **Nukutoso** (pronounced 'noo-koo-tor-sor', and meaning 'shifting sands'). In the second half of the 19th century, copra boosted the economy and drove development on the island. Nukutoso is one of the few plantations to survive from that time. Here, the copra is cut, dried, transported to the mill and processed into oil. Tours of the plantation are available.

For another rewarding outing, take the main road leading from Savusavu to Labasa for 50 minutes to the **Waisali Rainforest** (open Mon–Sat 8am–5pm; tel: 851 0939; admission fee), a flora and fauna reserve with a scenic walkway. The landscape is dramatic: ridges clad with dense rainforest soar skywards. Near the walkway entrance is the **Duiloma-loma Scenic Lookout**, where the view stretches down through a series of ranges opening out at Savusavu Bay. The entrance to the walkway is signalled by three small *bure*-style shelters, a couple of picnic tables and a large sign.

Take a picnic lunch, plus a swimsuit if you fancy a dip in the rainforest's water hole. This moist environment is home to two species of Fijian frog, the common ground frog and the tree frog. Be warned, the 1km (⅗-mile) circular trek through the rainforest involves steep downhill and uphill sections. The stone walkway is edged with handrails in the most difficult sections. The downhill part ends at a small waterfall that has been dammed to create a water hole for swimming. This is also a good place for a picnic and a rest before making the uphill return journey. The bush is cooling, and the chorus of cicadas, tree frogs and wood pigeons is, at times, deafening. The walk takes about 50 minutes, but allow longer if you want to stop and enjoy a swim and a picnic.

It's best to go on a tour or take a guide to reach **Nakawage Waterfall and Caves**. The turn-off from the Savusavu–

Bringing home the bacon, Vanua Levu

Labasa road is not signposted, and only a small sign and chained entranceway indicate where the walk to the falls begins. The walk is a moderate climb of 15 minutes or so along a well-defined pathway. Handrails made from thin branches have been put in place in the trickiest sections. Overall, it's a beautiful walk and quite different from the one at Waisali. There is a tidy clearing near the waterfall with toilet facilities, and a concrete walkway is under construction.

Further along the minor road from Nakawage Waterfall and Caves you will find the **Nukubolu Hot Springs** and the ruins of the ancient village of **Nukubola**. This is an adventurous trip, with river crossings and some driving challenges.

If you get the opportunity, take a river ride up the nearby **Nasekawa River** (a tour can be organised through most resorts). Dense rainforest trees drip down into still waters, casting reflections that will long remain in your memory. The chances are that you may see locals moving downriver on a *bilibili*. The landscape has a primeval atmosphere, with peaks rising dramatically in the distance.

Two other trips from Savusavu should be considered. A 40km (25-mile) drive into the interior of the west of the island along the Wailevu West Road brings you to **Nakasa** (pronounced 'na-ka-sar'). There are panoramic views before you enter the rainforest and trek to a waterfall. It's best to do this trip as a tour because of the poor state of the road.

Back in Savusavu, a road runs along the coast to the southwest. After about 15km (9 miles) it comes to an end at the **Cousteau Resort** (<www.fijiresort.com>), a luxurious retreat on a 7-hectare (17-acre) coconut grove. The resort prides itself on catering for families, on blending traditional Fijian styles within a modern context, and on providing a romantic getaway. The resort was named number-one resort on *Condé Nast Traveler*'s Green List in 2005 for outstanding ecotourism.

The rainforest meets the sea on Taveuni

TAVEUNI

Taveuni (population 12,000) is known as the Garden Island because of its lush vegetation. It attracts nature-lovers, bird-watchers and scuba divers from around the globe. With its beaches, large stands of rainforest, a vast array of flora and fauna and arguably the finest soft-coral reefs in the world, Taveuni has something to satisfy a wide range of interests.

Located 144km (90 miles) northeast of Viti Levu and only 9km (5½ miles) from the southeasternmost point of Vanua Levu, Taveuni is easily accessible by air and boat. Air Fiji and Pacific Sun operate regular trips, but flights are often heavily booked. For those coming by plane, the aerial views are spectacular. The car ferry operated by Beach Comber Cruises transports vehicles to Taveuni from Savusavu on Vanua Levu, a five-hour trip, but there's no real advantage in taking your own vehicle, because you can hire a car on the island or use local taxis or buses.

Taveuni is 42km (26 miles) long and 10km (6 miles) wide. From the interior rise some of Fiji's highest peaks. **Des Voeux Peak** is 1,195m (3,944ft) high, and **Mount Uluigalau**, Fiji's second-highest summit, rises to 1,241m (4,095ft) and is often cloud-covered. The geography of the island is diverse: fringed with reef in the northeast; with deep water close to the shore in the southwest; a rugged eastern coast with dramatic waterfalls; and on the southern coast there are caves and blowholes.

The majority of tourist hotels, restaurants and dive shops are located at **Matei**, in the north of the island near the airport, and also around the village of **Somosomo**, near where the ferry lands, on the west coast. Take time to laze on tiny, pristine **Prince Charles Beach**, near Matei, a crescent of white sand with overhanging coconut palms – pure bliss.

At times Taveuni seems to be in a time warp. Villages have a subsistence economy and are still ruled by chiefs. Women wash clothes in streams, stopping to wave to the passing tourists. Electricity is supplied by generators, and coastal roads wander through coconut plantations. Roads are sealed around the main tourist areas; elsewhere the roads are narrow, dusty, potholed and winding.

The island's open-air buses are a cheap and convenient method of exploring wide areas of the island, and, so long as you don't mind squeezing into a tight space next to the locals, are great fun. Runs are sporadic, so check the timetable or ask at your accommodation.

Taxis are plentiful, but fares are about 10 times the bus fare. Most passenger-

Village scene, Taveuni

carrying vehicles can be identified by a yellow number plate. Taveuni taxi drivers make great guides, so give the driver a list of places you would like to visit, and negotiate a fee. Prices vary according to the length of the trip, from between F$110 and F$200 for a full-day tour. Sharing with other tourists is an economical option. A taxi company that offers personal tours is Mr Sukh and Sons (tel: 888 0517).

Western Taveuni

Somosomo is the largest village and seat of the Tui Cakau, Taveuni's 'king'. There's a large hall built for a 1987 meeting of the **Great Council of Chiefs**, a national body of hereditary rulers. Alongside it, the **William Cross Memorial Church** houses the grave of William Cross, a missionary who first recorded today's system of the written Fijian language. Heading south, Somosomo joins with **Naqara**, the main commercial centre, which has a few dingy shops, the island's only bank (the Colonial Bank) and a couple of tiny cafés.

The Legend of the Tagimaucia Flower

The beautiful tagimaucia flower is found only in the Taveuni interior, around Lake Tagimaucia, and all attempts to transplant the vine on which it grows have failed. There are many variations of the legend of how the tagimaucia flower came to be. Here is one of them.

High in the mountains of Taveuni a young village maiden fell in love with a poor young man. She didn't know she was already promised to an older, uglier but extremely rich man. When told, she fled into the rainforest where she became lost and entangled in vines. No matter how she struggled, she couldn't break free. She wept, and as her tears fell, they blossomed with red-and-white flowers. She was eventually found and freed by a search party, and allowed to marry her lover and live happily ever after.

At the southern end of Naqara is the trail that leads to an arduous hike 823m (2,715ft) up to **Lake Tagimaucia**, where from October to January visitors may be lucky enough to find the rare red-and-white tagimaucia flower *(see opposite)*.

Tagimaucia flower

The police station, government offices and hospital are on a hillside at **Waiyevo**, 4km (5½ miles) south of Somosomo. Here you will also find a point marking where the **180th Meridian** runs north–south through Taveuni. In the mid-19th century, the International Date Line ran along the meridian, which meant that one side of the island was one day ahead of the other. Opportunist European plantation owners with land straddling the line got their labourers to work seven days a week by moving them to whichever side of the line was not experiencing a Sunday, thus denying them a day off. An 1879 ordinance ended this by placing all of Fiji west of the line. Within walking distance of the meridian marker are the **Waitavala Sliding Rocks**, where local children play on a natural water slide of smooth rocks along which water cascades.

Taveuni's lush and colourful forests are paralleled below the waters by the spectacular coral reefs. In particular, the soft corals are some of the world's best. The fierce, nutrient-rich currents sweeping in and around the **Somosomo Strait** between Vanua Levu and Taveuni are responsible for the prolific stands of soft coral. **Rainbow Reef**, characterised by a rainbow-like array of soft corals, includes **The Great White**

Wall, a large vertical structure smothered in white soft corals. The corals look all the more magnificent as their fronds sweep back and forth in the strong currents. And, of course, there's a plethora of fish and other marine life.

Eastern Taveuni

The interior and eastern parts of the island are characterised by rugged rainforests, waterfalls and remote coastal areas. Rainfall is high, so if you visit this area, take wet-weather gear or an umbrella. **Bouma National Heritage Park** (Tavaro Waterfalls Visitors' Centre; open daily 9am–4pm; tel: 888 0390; admission fee), also known as **Tavoro Forest Park**, preserves some 15,000 hectares (37,000 acres) of Taveuni rainforest. The main access point is Tavoro Waterfalls Visitors' Centre, 45 minutes by bus from Matei. Some of the key attractions include the Vidawa Rainforest Hike, Waitabu Marine Park and the Lavena Coastal Walk. There are also three waterfalls immediately south of the village of Bouma, linked by a walking trail. Access to each falls gets progressively more difficult, but the falls are spectacular in full flow, and rest points offer dramatic views of **Qamea Island** and Taveuni's northeast coast.

Bouma waterfalls

The guided **Vidawa Rainforest Hike** (tel: 888 0451;

book at least 12 hours ahead) takes six hours. It visits archaeological sites and the locations of old villages, and gives access to spectacular vistas. Hikers may get a glimpse of the rare orange dove, among other species.

Waitabu Marine Park (tel: 888 0451; admission fee) protects a lagoon 2km (1¼ miles) north of Bouma. It was established in 1998 when seven Fijian communities agreed not to fish or anchor within 1km (⅔ mile) of certain fringing reefs. Snorkelling is the main activity; diving is not allowed. Tours can be arranged that include boat transfers, snorkelling and rides on *bilibilis*.

> A highlight of any rainforest walk is the sight of a flock of brightly coloured kula (collared lories) as they search the forest for pollen and nectar. Their brilliant red feathers were once prized as decorations, particularly as fringes on woven matting. Today, coloured strands of wool are used around the matting but are still referred to as *kula*.

Lavena Coastal Walk (admission fee payable at Lavena Lodge Visitors' Centre) is a relatively easy 5km (3-mile) hike of about an hour and a half – enough to get you hot and sweaty. It takes you down the Ravilevo Coast to Wainibau Falls, passing **Naba Village** – home to descendants of Solomon Islanders brought here in the 19th century to work on plantations – and across a suspension bridge over the **Wainisari River**, which drains **Lake Tagimaucia** in the interior. The narrow path hugs a coastline dense with plants and overhung with trees, reminiscent of a botanical garden where house plants have grown out of control to a gigantic stature. The idyllic beach of golden sand at the start of the walk was the location for the 1991 film *Return to the Blue Lagoon*. If long hikes are not your thing, you can also kayak the coastline and return by foot.

Kayaking off Fulanga Island, Lau Group

LAU GROUP

The Lau Group (also known as the Eastern Group) is made up of some 60 islands and atolls lying southeast of Vanua Levu and Viti Levu, and halfway between Fiji and Tonga. The group falls into two parts: Northern Lau and Southern Lau. **Vanua Balavu** (in Northern Lau) and **Lakeba** (in Southern Lau) are the most important islands. There is excellent diving and snorkelling, but little in the way of tourist facilities.

Air Fiji (tel: 331 3666) runs a weekly flight from Suva to Vanua Balavu; there are no scheduled flights to other parts of the Lau Group. Other than that, only charter boats, private yachts or the occasional cargo supply ship visit the islands. It is difficult to travel between islands.

Basic accommodation is available on Lakeba and Vanua Balavu on a guesthouse or village-stay basis. Kaimbu, a small, privately owned island to the west of Vanua Balavu, is an exclusive resort.

The Lau Group was ruled for a long time by Tongan chiefs, and there is still a strong Tongan influence, both culturally and physically, especially in Southern Lau, where the people are fairer-skinned than most Fijians and the language is a mixture of Fijian and Tongan. The villages feature traditional thatched houses that are round-shaped in the Tongan style rather than square-shaped as in other parts of Fiji. The Lauans are expert carvers, making bowls with intricate inlaid patterns in mother-of-pearl, and are also renowned for their design work on *masi*.

Some islands are extinct volcanoes, some are coral atolls, while others are limestone, with rugged hills and extensive cave systems; coral reefs lie offshore. Human interference has been low, so the waters are in a near-pristine state. On the reefs, coral gardens, huge sea fans and large patches of cabbage coral make a spectacular sight, and with virtually no river run-off from the islands, the water is extremely clear. Schools of pelagic fish patrol the waters, along with many other large species, including sharks, barracuda and sailfish. All of this makes the Lau Group a diver's paradise, but the lack of land-based professional diving services means that would-be divers are limited to snorkelling, unless they explore the islands on a live-aboard dive boat like the *Naia* (<www.naia.com.fj>), *Tui Tai* (<www.tuitai.com>) or *Fiji Aggressor* (<www.fijiaggressor.com>).

The islands may be remote, but they have produced more than their share of notable and highly respected Fijians. Ratu Sir Kamisese Mara was hereditary paramount chief of the Lau islands, prime minister mainly between 1967 and 1992, and president from 1993 to 2000. Another Lauan, Laisenia Qarase, was Fiji's prime minister at the time of the 2006 coup.

Vanua Balavu

Vanua Balavu is an elongated island of 53 sq km (20 sq miles). It is characterised by steep, undercut cliffs and fertile volcanic soil, hot springs and, offshore, an extensive reef system that includes the islets of **Qiliqila Bay** (the Bay of Islands). The island has a copra port and a small hospital. **Lomaloma** is the largest village.

Vanua Balavu is the most accessible of the Lau islands and is a mecca for yachtsmen. Qilaqila Bay (pronounced 'gillag-illa'), at the northern end, is reputed to be one of the best yacht harbours in the South Pacific. The tiny limestone islands, archways and fallen arches that litter the bay create a kayaker's fantasy seascape. The island also has plenty of pleasant sandy bays and superb snorkelling. Don't expect to have a raging time. Lomaloma has two shops, a bakery and a post office, and there are no bars, clubs, restaurants or banks; hard cash is the only currency. The islanders are staunch churchgoers, and the singing at Sawana Tongan Church on Sundays is a highlight.

Lakeba

Lakeba is roughly circular in shape, and has a land area of 59 sq km (23 sq miles) and a population of 2,100 in eight villages, of which Tubou is the main one. A 29km (18-mile) road encircles the island. It is known for its caves, the most famous of which is **Oso Nabukete** or the Pregnant Woman's Cave. According to legend, any woman trying to hide her pregnancy will be unable to escape through the mouth of the cave. Adjoining it is **Oara Bulu**, which once served as a prison during tribal wars. A third cave, **Koro ni Vono**, was the final resting place for tuberculosis sufferers. A guide from Nasaqalau Village willingly escorts you to these places. Make sure you bring a *sevusevu* for the chief, and a good torch.

Nasaqalau Village is known for its clan's ability to call sharks. This ceremony is conducted by a *bete* (Fijian traditional priest) during October or November. Offerings of kava are made in the days leading up to the ceremony. On the chosen day a shark caller wades neck-high into the water, chanting loudly. If all goes according to plan, a white shark will appear with a school of smaller grey sharks, which are caught while their leader goes free.

Archaeological excavations on the island in the 1990s uncovered the remains of an **ancient fortress**, large enough to house around 2,500 people. It may have been built to safeguard the population during Tongan invasions.

Other Islands

Fulanga is a coral atoll in Southern Lau shaped like a narrow crescent. It is low-lying, being only 80m (260ft) above sea level at its highest point. Around the lagoon are islets that have been sculpted into mushroom shapes by wind and wave action. Fulanga is one of the last places in Fiji where sailing outrigger canoes are still built, and where wind power is favoured over petrol.

Fulanga, Lau Group

Moala is the largest member of the **Moala Group**, which lies about midway between Kadavu and Southern Lau. Moala and the two other islands in the group – Totoya and Matuku – have no tourism infrastructure, and there are no scheduled flights. The only accommodation option is to arrange to stay with a local family.

WHAT TO DO

It would be easy for visitors to do nothing except revel in the lazy ambience of Fiji's tropical climate, swing in a hammock, read a book or cool off in the ocean. These are all reasons why tourists choose Fiji as a holiday destination. But Fiji also lends itself to all manner of outdoor pursuits, from placid to hardcore adventure. You can raft white-water rivers, dive in deep blue seas and explore rainbow-coloured reefs, dance with locals on a balmy night or, enshrouded in mountain mist, wait patiently for a fleeting glimpse of a rare bird.

OUTDOOR PURSUITS

Watersports

Scuba Diving and Snorkelling. Fiji is one of the world's best diving and snorkelling locations, and is especially known for its diversity of multicoloured soft corals. But there are hard corals, too, as well as all manner of sealife, from tiny anemone fish and well-camouflaged molluscs to sharks, manta rays, dolphins and even whales. And three of the world's seven turtle species return to Fiji's sandy beaches to lay their eggs.

You can dive year-round, but July to November is the best period for settled weather. Underwater visibility begins at around 15m (50ft) and can reach 45m (150ft) in places. Water temperature varies from 24°C (75°F) in June, July and August to 30°C (86°F) in December, January and February. Each area has diving characteristics that are unique to its location. On Viti Levu and its offshore islands, the Mamanuca

Soft-coral garden at Taveuni

Coral reef etiquette: don't touch the coral with your feet, hands or equipment if you can help it; don't collect animals, plants or coral, or buy them as souvenirs unless you know their collection is managed on a sustainable basis.

and Yasawa groups, barrier reefs protect shallow lagoons, which along the Coral Coast are close to the shoreline in places. Beqa and Vatulele have passages, sea mounts and large underwater boulders (bommies), while the northern islands, including Taveuni, have some of the most famous dive sites in the world, including Rainbow Reef and the Great White Wall *(see pages 73–4)*. In central Fiji (Lomaiviti and Ra), vast current-flushed reef systems remain largely unexplored. In Kadavu there are deep walls and shallow reef-garden grottoes, while off Savusavu, on Vanua Levu, there are more than 20 recognised dive sites.

Many of Fiji's great dives are close to resorts, most of which have facilities recognised by the Professional Association of Diving Instructors (PADI). Some offer dive training. For more information on diving, see <www.divefiji.com>.

Surfing. Fiji's surf breaks attract surfers from around the world, and most are definitely not for the novice. Legendary breaks include Cloudbreak, a 6m (20ft) wave that breaks off Tavarua Island. It featured in the 1994 movie *The Endless Summer 2.* Well-known breaks on or near Viti Levu can be reached by boat. There are a few shore breaks. Natadola Beach on the Coral Coast is good for body-boarding and beginner surfers, but watch out for the strong undertow. Sigatoka, also on the Coral Coast, is another good spot for beginners.

Several resorts and camps have been established for surfers, notably on Beqa and Yanuca islands. Batiluvu in Beqa Lagoon provides easy access to Frigate Passage, a premier surf location and one of the most consistent in terms of swell. The Passage has a left-hand break that rolls over a relatively smooth coral reef; rides of 100m (330ft) or more are not uncommon.

Surfers need to take their own boards, so ask your airline about baggage restrictions, and note that local airlines demand advance warning if you are bringing a board. You can surf throughout the year, with the best swells out of the south from March to October. Fiji's surfing competitions are both held at Tavarua: the Rip Curl Oceania Surfing Cup in January and the Quiksilver Pro in May. For more information on surfing, see <www.globalsurfers.com/fiji.cfm>.

Windsurfing. Conditions for windsurfing are excellent in the Mamanuca Group and the Sigatoka area of Viti Levu. Windsurfers can be hired at many resorts.

Kite surfing. This sport is becoming increasingly popular in areas such as Ellington Wharf near Rakiraki on Viti Levu,

Preparing to dive

Kayaking into the sunset

where equipment, tuition and accommodation are available (Safari Lodge; tel: 948 8888 or 669 3333; <www.safari lodge.com.fj>).

Kayaking. Kayaking is an ideal way to experience Fiji's small islands and stunning coastline fully. The unobtrusive nature of paddling means you get close to unique ecosystems, whether they be mangrove forests or coral lagoons. Different types of craft available include scuba kayaks, built to carry scuba equipment; sit-on-top models; and single and double sea kayaks with room for storage on longer excursions. Popular sea-kayaking destinations include the Yasawa Group and Kadavu, which have convoluted coastlines to explore and plenty of places to go ashore. Several companies offer organised trips from one to seven days, usually in the dry season between May and November. One of the leading sea-kayaking companies is Tamarillo Tropical Expeditions (<www.seakayakfiji.com>).

Jetboating. Jetboating is an exhilarating way to explore mangrove-lined tidal corridors. Trips operated by Jet Fiji (tel: 675 0400; <www.jetfiji.com>) depart every 15 minutes from Port Denarau, 7km (4 miles) from Nadi, for a 30-minute blast along the Nadi River. Drivers intersperse their narration of local culture and history with jaw-dropping 360-degree spins. Jet Fiji also operates from various other locations.

Rafting. Rafting is an invigorating way to experience the interior of Viti Levu. Rafting rivers include the Rewa, Luva and the Upper Navua Gorge. A reasonable level of fitness is required, especially for rafters opting for full-day or overnight expeditions. Boats are equipped to handle crews of four to six with training and full safety briefings prior to departure.

Rafting companies also use **inflatable rafts** for single paddlers and offer **bamboo rafting** (referred to locally as a *bilibili* ride). In Viti Levu villagers will pole you through the Waiqa Gorge on a bamboo raft from Naitauvoli to Naivucini villages. A leading rafting operator is Rivers Fiji (tel: 345 0147; <www.riversfiji.com>).

Fishing

With so many islands surrounded by so much water, it would be hard not to catch a fish in Fiji. You can try your hand at **saltwater fly-fishing** in the Tavewa, Nacula islands and surrounding areas of the Yasawas, but **game-fishing** is the main focus of attention. Species include blue, black and striped marlin, Spanish mackerel and skipjack tuna. Fishing charters off Viti Levu are based at Denarau Marina in Nadi and at Pacific Harbour on the south coast.

Popular fishing locations are around Beqa and Kadavu, the north coast of Taveuni and around the Mamanuca Group. Many resorts in these areas have their own fishing boats.

Charter operators provide a guide service, boat and gear, and most will have negotiated fishing rights with local villages. Many operators encourage a 'catch-and-release' policy on all billfish and other game fish not destined for the dinner plate.

Fishing is possible all year, but many game species have a best season: wahoo from May to August; billfish from March to April, July to August and October to November; tanguige from February to April, July to August and October to November; and tuna from April to July. Sailfish occur throughout the year, but are possibly best in August. Pacific Harbour hosts Fiji's annual game-fishing tournament in August. For more information on game-fishing in Fiji, see <www.sportfishingfiji.com>.

Cruising and Sailing

Various cruise operators depart from Denarau for daily trips to different destinations in the Mamanuca Group. Cruises include time for watersports, coral-viewing, fish-feeding, beach barbecues and sunbathing. Cruises to the Yasawas, which depart from Lautoka, need to be booked, and are generally longer than those to the Mamanucas (Blue Lagoon Cruises; tel: 666 1622; <www.bluelagooncruises.com>). A complete cruise package – in which you live aboard the ship, with all meals and activities included in the price – allows you to travel in style and explore Fiji's outer, less readily accessible islands.

Those with some sailing experience can hire a catamaran or small yacht at some resorts. If you fancy something more ambitious, consider chartering a yacht. Musket Cove Yacht Club, on the island of Malololailai in the Mamanucas, has

Sailing a catamaran

a range of different-sized yachts available for charter (tel: 651 2215; <www.musketcovefiji.com>). Note that Fijian law dictates that a local guide is present on all chartered vessels.

For complete adventure, book a berth on the *Tui Tai* (tel: 885 3032; <www.tuitai.com>), a tall-masted ship that sails from Savusavu and cruises along the coast of

Vanua Levu. Guests can go ashore at various places and use the kayaks, mountain bikes and other adventure equipment carried on board. The ship also offers scuba-diving expeditions.

Hiking and Biking

A walk in a rainforest can be a cooling relief from the humidity of Fiji's urban areas. Walks vary in length and nature and may be guided or independent. The National Trust of Fiji administers six national parks, all with trails. **Koroyanitu National Park** *(see page 37)*, has day and overnight walks. One circular trail leads into the rainfor-

Hiking on Taveuni

est, through banyan tree forests to a high waterfall and returns along the open grassy ridges of surrounding hills. The park is within the Nausori Highlands, which has impressive rolling hills, river valleys and volcanic peaks. Walkers are treated to views of the Mamanuca and southern Yasawa islands.

The **Sigatoka Sand Dunes National Park** *(see page 44)*, on the south coast of Viti Levu, has a choice of walking trails. **Colo-i-Suva Forest Park** *(see page 54)*, less than 20 minutes' drive from Suva, has 6km (4 miles) of rainforest trails. The area has several small waterfalls, indigenous flora and bird life, and scenic lookouts.

Three separate hikes in **Bouma National Heritage Park** on Taveuni *(see page 74)* include **Tavoro Waterfalls**, the

Lavena Coastal Walk and the **Vidawa Rainforest Hike**. A guide is highly recomended for the latter walk, and is essential for the arduous trek to **Lake Tagimaucia**.

On the hilly, grass-covered island of **Waya** in the Yasawa islands, scenic trails give dramatic views over high coastal ridges. On Ovalau, there are excellent trails on the peaks behind Levuka; serious hikers might consider the trek to **Lovoni Village** in the centre of the island.

In many places there are shorter walks that are suited to less active travellers. A good example is The Garden of the Sleeping Giant (*see page 28*) outside Nadi.

Walking Stick Adventures organise **mountain-biking** excursions through the Sleeping Giant Region (tel: 672 4673; <www.walkingstickadventures.com>). On Vanua Levu, there are good mountain-bike trails around the island's western roads; bikes are available from Trip n' Tours (tel: 885 3154; email: <tripntours@connect.com.fj>) in Savusavu.

Birdwatching

The rainforests of Taveuni and Kadavu are renowned for their rare and beautiful birds, and are a magnet for ornithologists. Species include kula and kadavu parrots, orange doves, wattled honey-eaters and kingfishers. An excellent site on Taveuni is Des Voeux Peak, reached by four-wheel drive followed by a few hours' hiking. Some of Fiji's rare rainforest species have been spotted here. Guided walks are available with a local guide known as Boro. His reputation for experience and knowledge in this field is unsurpassed. Contact him through Garden Island Resort, or tel: 888 0625 or 948 2235.

On Viti Levu, Colo-i-Suva Forest Park, near Suva, is a good birdwatching destination. For closer observation of species cared for in well-designed aviaries, visit **Kula Eco Park**, a short ride from Pacific Harbour.

Red-footed boobie, Namenalala Island

On **Namenalala Island**, 40km (25 miles) from Savusavu, birdwatchers can get close to red-footed boobies, Polynesian starlings and white-tailed tropic birds. It's an extraordinary experience to sit at the clifftop tip of the island and watch seabirds ride the wind, seemingly within arm's length. The island is the preserve of guests of Moody's Namena resort.

Golf

Except for the most humid months, Fiji's climate is perfect for this sport. Many upmarket resorts have their own private courses, and there are championship golf courses at the Denarau Golf Club, Pacific Harbour Country Club and Fiji Golf Club on Viti Levu, along with smaller public courses. (Vanua Levu and Taveuni also have one course each.)

Top Fijian golfer Vijay Singh won the PGA Championship in 1998 and 2004. Several professional and Pro-Am Competitions are held annually, including the Shangri-La Fijian Resort

Pro-Am, BMW International Charity Pro-Am and Air New Zealand Invitational Pro-Am – all in May – and Fiji Bitter Open, Pacific Harbour Pro-Am and Denarau Pro-Am, in June.

Denarau Golf and Racquet Club, a 10-minute drive from Nadi town, is open to the public. A round of golf with compulsory golf cart costs F$105.

SHOPPING

There's no shortage of shops in Suva, Nadi or along the Coral Coast, but for the genuine article and a cultural experience visit the **municipal markets** (open Mon–Sat) held in all the larger centres. Fijians produce excellent **carved items**, including bowls, clubs, spears and cannibal forks (three-pronged wooden forks used by cannibals to eat human flesh). On jewellery stalls you'll find a wide selection of locally made **shell necklaces** and earrings, but cheap imported jewellery is beginning to make an appearance. There's an abundance of *masi* (*tapa* **cloth**) in a variety of sizes, and woven items, such as mats, baskets, trays, purses and fans. Many woven goods available in Savusavu are woven from *kuta*, a locally grown reed specific to Vanua Levu. The fibre is finer than pandanus and slightly glossier. Buying articles from the markets nearly always ensures you get an item particular to that area, and in remoter areas some items even appear to be slightly used. Buy traditional **clay pots** and **crockery** from pottery villages along the Sigatoka River.

Carvers use a variety of woods, including coconut shell. If purchasing wooden items, keep in mind that in some countries they may have to be declared at Customs; shells and items made from rare or endangered animals are automatically confiscated and destroyed.

Souvenirs and artefacts can be purchased from almost identical stores in Nadi or Suva. Jack's Handicrafts, Nada's and Sogo's are boutique tourist shops, with outlets in major centres and most larger resorts. Shops are generally air-conditioned, always a bonus in a humid climate. The official government crafts centre at Ratu Sukuna House on Carnarvon Sreet, Suva, has a good range of genuine items.

Black pearls cultivated in Savusavu Bay *(page 65)* can be purchased at various locations around Fiji, but the best place is the J. Hunter Pearls showroom in Savusavu. If you can't afford the alluring pearl rings, necklaces or sets of jewellery with price tags up to F$22,000, ask to see the trays of pearls behind the counter, and choose your own from around F$40.

The main centres have numerous shops selling **electronic and duty-free goods**: cameras, televisions, watches, binoculars, clocks, lighters, hi-fi equipment, perfumes, pewter, crystal and porcelain. Shopkeepers will often give discounts on large purchases. Small, inexpensive gifts include **coconut oils and soap** made in Fiji, and **spices** (pepper, ginger, cinnamon and cardamom), which are often packaged in pottery or locally made containers.

Clothes-manufacturing is a major industry, and shops stock a wide range of shirts, dresses and *sulu* (sarongs) – all inexpensive and good quality. Tailors and seamstresses will quickly stitch together something in your size and to your own requirements for a reasonable fee.

Bargaining at the market

A *meke* in full swing

ENTERTAINMENT

Cultural Entertainment

You'd go a long way to beat the excitement of a *meke* (traditional song and dance), firewalking exhibition or Fijian theatre for entertainment. The Arts Village, Pacific Habour *(see page 47)*, and **Ka Levu South Pacific Cultural Centre** on the Coral Coast (tel: 652 0200; <http://fijicultural centre.com>; admission fee) stage lively demonstrations of firewalking, mock fighting, storytelling, singing, dancing, music, costume and drama.

Most major resorts organise weekly *meke*. If you happen to visit a local school, you may be rewarded with a spontaneous performance (a donation is politely and gratefully accepted). There's a full-time Indian Cultural Centre showcasing Indian dance, theatre and music at the **Girmit Centre**, Lautoka.

Nightlife

If energetic nightlife is what you want, you can find it in most main centres. Suva's Victoria Parade comes alive at night with bars, clubs and eateries. Among them is **Traps Back Bar** (six bars in one), thronged with teenagers, twenty-somethings, expats, members of the business élite and tourists. **Reilly's**, an Irish-themed pub with a wraparound bar in the centre, is nearby. Thursday is reputed to be the liveliest night of the week, followed by Friday and Saturday. **Purple Haze**, a Bollywood-themed nightclub on McArthur Street, is a draw with the Indian population, but most bars and clubs attract a good mix.

It's not uncommon to find Fijians in a club sharing local beer from a jug using a single glass passed among the group, a practice that probably evolved from the *yaqona* ceremony where a *bilo* (half a coconut shell) of *yaqona* or grog is passed around. The minimum age is 18, and you

---

Meke

It's a rare Fijian who can't sing or dance. Their sense of rhythm and expert harmony are enviable. *Meke* are a combination of song, dance and drama performed at feasts, on special occasions and at the tourist hotels. Performers paint their faces and wear skirts made from shredded leaves, or colourful *sulusulu*, and hang floral lei round their necks.

Both men and women do the *vakamalolo*, a sitting dance, but it is women who dance the *seasea* with fans, while men perform rousing war dances that evoke Fiji's violent past. You'll be mesmerised by the colourful spectacle, but be warned, you won't get away with just watching. At some stage you'll be pulled to your feet to join in the *tralala*, a simple two-foot shuffle which even an inept or inebriated tourist can manage.

need proof of age and photo identification. Dress is casual, but no flip-flops or shorts. Clubs with live music will request a cover charge.

Those travellers wanting a more sedate time might enjoy a drink at the older colonial clubs in safe and friendly surroundings. These places are also good sources of local news and information. They often display a Members Only sign, but foreigners are allowed entry provided they adhere to the dress code.

Cinemas are popular, and can be found in most major towns. Fiji's first feature film, *The Land Has Eyes*, directed by Vilsoni Hereniko, had its world première in 2004 at Sundance and was subsequently nominated for an Oscar. The film, a powerful and moving tale of a young Rotuman woman inspired and haunted by a warrior woman from her island's mythology, was filmed on the island of Rotuma (600km/375 miles from Viti Levu), and almost all the cast were local actors, many of whom had never been to a cine-

---

Weddings

Getting hitched in Fiji is becoming increasingly popular. Resorts, hotels and cruises offer wedding and honeymoon packages, ranging from traditional white – riding in on white horses – to traditional Fijian – paddled ashore by a team of warriors. Every aspect of organisation is taken care of, right down to the singing.

To get married in Fiji you'll need: original birth certificate and passport for both of you; consent from parent or guardian, officially witnessed, if you're under 21; decree absolute (divorce papers) if relevant; death certificate of any former spouse now deceased.

Present yourselves together at a registry office in Fiji to apply for the licence, which can be issued within one working day. There are registry offices in Suva, Nadi, Sigatoka and Lautoka.

ma. Several other movies have been shot in or around Fiji, including *The Blue Lagoon* and *Anaconda*. Fiji's Indian population embraces Bollywood.

Rugby

The Fijians are only second to New Zealanders in their passion for rugby. If you get the opportunity, go to a local match. Games are hard-fought, and the atmosphere electric. You won't meet many tourists, and it's a great way to be involved with Fijian exuberance. Bring a towel to sit on and buy local snacks such as barbecued meat and curry in roti.

Rugby match, Sigatoka

CHILDREN'S FIJI

Children enjoy Fiji and Fijians love children, so it's a great destination for introducing children to a different culture, where the climate and outdoor activities will keep them fully occupied. Many resorts are specifically geared to family entertainment, especially those in the Mamanuca Group, such as **Plantation Island**, **Beachcomber Island**, **Treasure Islands** and **Musket Cove**. Independent programmes are run during the day: basket-weaving, coconut-husking, pool games and beachcombing. The evening entertainment often morphs into the night, beginning with activities suitable for younger children, such as **crab racing** and **bingo**, and progressing to **karaoke** or **disco** for the teenagers. Menus also cater for whimsical appetites.

Full nanny services are available at most locations, and the happy, patient dispositions of most Fijian women make them ideal for this position. Charges are reasonable.

Kula Eco Park *(see page 46),* near Pacific Harbour on Viti Levu, has a special environmental education centre. Getting close to indigenous wildlife will create indelible memories for you and your children.

Island-hopping by boat, a trip on the **Coral Coast Railway** or a **horse ride** along Natadola Beach are all good ways for children to appreciate the landscape. The **Fiji Museum** has items that appeal to children's ghoulish sense of humour, including cannibal ovens and eating utensils, breastplates and weapons. One war club used in battle has grooves cut into it indicating the number of enemy killed.

On the island of Nananu-i-Ra *(see page 40),* a 10-minute boat ride off the northern coast of Viti Levu, there are self-catering cabins, sheltered beaches, safe swimming and good conditions for children to

A first dive

snorkel and **kayak**. **Kids Sea Camp** (<www.kidssea camp.com>), a children's holiday programme endorsed by the Professional Association of Diving Instructors (PADI), has chosen Fiji as a camp destination. Children learn snorkelling, diving and fish identification, and are encouraged to develop love and respect for the ocean.

Calendar of Events

January: Rip Curl Oceania Surfing Cup, Tavarua Island; Thaipusam (Hindu ceremony), Nadi Temple.

February/March: Hindu Holi (Festival of Colours) – a big event in Lautoka, where people bombard each other with coloured water.

March/April: Ram Naumi (Birth of Lord Rama), Hindu religious festival: a big event in Suva Bay, where locals wade into the water and through flowers.

April: Fiji International Jazz Festival, on the Coral Coast; Auckland to Musket Cove Yacht Rally, Mamanuca.

May: Numerous golf tournaments, including: Shangri-La's Fijian Resort Pro-Am; BMW International Charity Pro-Am and Air New Zealand Invitational Pro-Am – all held at Denarau Golf Club, Denarau Island, near Nadi. Also Quiksilver Pro Surfing Competition, Tavarua Island.

June: Golf: Fiji Bitter Open, Pacific Harbour Pro-Am and the Denarau Pro-Am. International Bula Marathon – held near Sigatoka.

July: Bula Festival, Nadi – the city's main celebration.

July/August: Hibiscus Festival, Suva – parades, marching bands and beauty pageants.

August: Fiji Ocean Swim – swimmers from around the world tackle a 3.2km (2-mile) or 1.5km (1-mile) ocean course over reefs off Mana Island Resort. Hindu Firewalking – Howell Road, Suva.

September: Fiji Regatta Week and the Musket Cove to Port Vila Yacht Race (<www.musketcovefiji.com>) – yachts from around the world converge on Musket Cove. Sugar Festival, Lautoka – celebrates the town's major industry with parades and other fun activities.

October: Back to Levuka Festival, Ovalau – parades and ceremonies.

October/November: Diwali (Festival of Lights) – candles and lanterns are placed in doorways and windows in honour of Lakshmi, goddess of wealth and prosperity. Bilibili Race, Sigatoka – friendly, fun-filled racing on traditional bamboo rafts down the Sigatoka River.

November: South Pacific World Music Festival, Savusavu – with Fijian and international musicians.

December: New Year's Eve Street Party, Suva – street dancing.

EATING OUT

Wherever you go out to eat in Fiji you'll find plenty of European dishes, but for an unforgettable culinary experience, go instead for the local Fijian, Indian and Chinese cuisine, and creative blends of these. Often it's not only what you eat but where and how. Taste pineapple from a roadside stall, juice dripping down your chin. Take away a neatly wrapped banana leaf containing something unrecognisable yet tasty at the Lautoka market for later consumption. Drink green coconut milk in a swaying hammock under the palms, or dress up to dine out on the beach at sunset. If you do want to stay with European cuisine, restaurants attached to upmarket resorts offer classic dishes presented with style. No matter where you eat, the dress code is normally casual but tidy.

The *balolo*, a small marine worm, is considered to be a delicacy. On two nights of the year, one in October, the other in November, the *balolo* rises to the ocean's surface to mate, releasing its 'tail', which contains its eggs or sperm. Villagers go out at sunrise to scoop up millions of writhing tails, soaking them in fresh water before they are cooked overnight in a *lovo*. Ovalau in the Lomaiviti Group is the best place to observe this phenomenon.

Traditional Food

Fiji's climate is ideal for growing fruit and vegetables. Many Fijians tend their own gardens with great care, selling the produce to markets or local restaurants – mainly root crops such as **taro**, **yam**, **cassava** and **sweet potato**, but also fruits such as **mangoes**, **bananas** and **pawpaw** (papaya). The leaves of the taro plant are also used. And then, of course, there is the incomparable **coconut**.

Preparing the *lovo*

If you get invited to join a Fijian family for a meal or are present for an authentic Fijian celebration, you'll probably find yourself sitting cross-legged on a woven mat on the floor. As the honoured guest you'll be fed before the women and children, and given a generous serving of the best food, and the members of the household will watch closely as you eat it all.

Typically, there are two dishes: a main dish *(kakana dina)* of meat, fish or root vegetables grated and prepared in some palatable manner, and a side dish *(icoi)* of leafy vegetable or something complementary to the main dish.

Fijian cooking is based on one kind or another of starchy root vegetables – cassava, taro, breadfruit or yams – served with fish, shellfish, pork or chicken and a green vegetable such as taro leaves. Not much is used in the way of seasoning, maybe lemon juice or hot chillies. The majority of restaurants include a small selection of Fijian main dishes on their daily menu, and will have one night dedicated to traditional Fijian cuisine.

Favourite Fijian specialities include: *kokoda* (fish or other seafood marinated in lemon juice and coconut milk), *rourou* (a taro-leaf dish), *kassaua* (tapioca, often boiled, baked or grated, and cooked in coconut cream with sugar and mashed bananas), *duruka* (an unusual vegetable resembling asparagus, in season during April and May) and *paulsami* (baked taro leaves marinated in lemon juice and coconut milk, sometimes with a meat or fish filling and added onion or garlic).

You haven't experienced Fiji unless you have participated in a *lovo*. This traditional method of cooking is by underground oven. A large pit is dug in the earth and lined with dry coconut husks. The husks are set on fire and coral stones placed on top. When the flames die down and the stones are fully heated, food wrapped in banana leaves or

Yum yum! Parrot fish and bêche-de-mer

placed in woven baskets is placed on the stones – meat and fish first, followed by vegetables. The food is covered with leaves and wet sacks, and finally with a layer of dirt or sand. Then it's left to cook for approximately two hours.

Bêche-de-mer, the sea cucumber, is sold in dried form at local markets. Despite its unattractive appearance, it is also exported as a delicacy, mostly to the Japanese market.

The gathering, preparation and cooking of food is central to most communal gatherings. *Lovo* are not just for the tourists but paramount to all special occasions, such as weddings, festivals and the ceremonial welcome given to a new chief.

If you are staying in a coastal village you may get the chance to take part in a ***yarayara*** (fish drive). The villagers stand in a circle in deep water, up to the waist or chest, holding a rope or thick vine between them. They will shake this and beat sticks on the water to scare the fish into the centre. The women duck under the rope, catch a fish in a net, and bite its head to kill it.

Eating Indian

You're transported somewhere elusive and exotic when you enter the dark, atmospheric décor, smells and tastes of Fiji's many small Indian cafés and restaurants.

The popularity of Indian food means you'll find a wide range of curries and other dishes to sample on a typical menu. **Curries** are good value, offering an inexpensive, filling meal. They generally come with **dahl** (a cooked dish of lentils and spices), **roti** (a pancake of wheat flour cooked on a grill) or rice. Make sure you let the cook or waiter know what strength you like your curry. Be conservative: you can always make it hotter with a paste. The local Indian food is slightly different to that found on the Subcontinent, owing to the fact that the

Indians have been in Fiji long enough to create their own mix of dishes that incorporate Fijian ingredients, for example coconut milk. (Culinary influences also work in the other direction – Fijians spice their relishes with curry.)

Though curries obviously characterise Indian cuisine, other dishes from the Subcontinent are also popular: **idly** (dumplings), **masala dosa** (a rice pancake served with coconut sauce), as well as roti. Menus include vegetable, mutton, goat, chicken, pork and beef curries. For religious reasons, Muslims do not eat pork and Hindus do not eat beef.

If you happen to be invited to an Indo-Fijian home for a meal, it will be a genuine offer and a memorable experience. Indo-Fijian families usually eat together, but if the occasion is deemed formal you might find yourself fed first, with your hosts and other guests waiting until you have finished before they start eating.

Beachside meal

Other Cuisines

The popularity of **Chinese restaurants** is increasing in the main urban centres of Fiji. However, menus tend to be limited to well-known dishes such as fried rice, chop suey and chow mein.

A few **Japanese restaurants** have recently opened in the cities. They make the most of the fresh seafood so readily available.

Seafood

Surrounded as Fiji is by the Pacific, it's no wonder that fish and other seafoods are top of the menu for visitors. *Kokoda* is a favourite and can be selected as an entrée or main course. There are the usual pan-fried or baked fish fillets, but perhaps the best ways to eat the local fish are baked whole on a barbecue or in a *lovo*.

Fruit for sale

Fish in coastal areas are often small but rich in flavour. It's not uncommon to see fish stalls by the roadside near Rakiraki. Strings of reef fish and crabs are held out on display to passing cars and tempt you to stop. The stallholder is kept busy waving banana leaves over the fish to keep the flies away.

Markets also have fish stalls that are well worth a visit if you don't mind the smell.

Fruit and Vegetable Markets

You will see multicultural Fiji at its most engaging when you visit a market, and those in the Nadi and Lautoka areas are especially good, buzzing with activity. Fijians and Indians exchange gossip as they set out their stalls, then entice buyers with a cacophony of chants, bargaining, calls, whistles and laughter in Fijian, Hindi and English. Stalls are a blaze of colour, with their stacks of mangoes, pawpaw, lemons, bananas, guava, melon, passion fruit, etc.; sacks of spices, chillies and prepared curries; and tables laid out with crabs, prawns, seaweeds and sea grapes (a type of seaweed). There's all manner of foods to buy and try: delicacies wrapped in banana leaves, neatly peeled pineapples in spiral patterns, mouth-watering slices of pink melon and pots of curried dishes. Sights, sounds, smells and flavours together make for a memorable sensory experience.

Meat

A range of chicken, pork, beef and other meat dishes are available at Fiji's restaurants and other eateries. However, the majority of Fijians don't commonly eat meat because it is comparatively expensive. Instead, meat is reserved for a large celebration or feast.

Roadside Stalls

Roadside stalls sell fruit, vegetables and green coconuts. They also sell *roti* stuffed with curried meat or vegetables, a healthy, tasty, convenient and inexpensive takeaway snack. However, if the roti contain meat, be sure to ask how long they've been on display. It's best not to take any risks, although in most cases the food is fresh.

Takeaway goodies might also come wrapped in banana leaves. Inside could be grated and baked *tavioka* (cassava) and coconut, or some other vegetable mixture. Be adventurous and ready for a tasty surprise.

Kava Etiquette

When you visit a village, take some *yaqona* (the root of the pepper plant). You can buy the root at any market wrapped in bundles priced from F$10 to F$15. Remember that you are part of the ceremony, not watching it, so don't take photos during a formal ceremony. If you don't like kava (highly likely), at least try to finish the first offering. Tip the cup to show you have finished. Don't turn your back on the chief during the ceremony or walk in front of the circle of people. Don't step over the cord attached to the *tanoa* (the wooden bowl that contains the kava).

Kava ceremony in the chief's bure, Navala

Kava Culture

Kava, it goes without saying, is the most popular and widely drunk beverage in Fiji. Kava is more than just a drink – it's a culture, and one you must experience.

Kava is made from *yaqona*, the dried root *(waka)* of the pepper plant, *Macropiper methysticum*. (*Yaqona* is another name for the drink itself.) Kava is a tranquillising, non-alcoholic drink that numbs the tongue and lips and relaxes the imbiber. Kava is unpleasant in both appearance – it looks like dirty water – and taste, but drinking it is an integral part of Fijian culture, in which just about everything starts around a kava bowl. Even on informal occasions, there's a strict protocol for its use. Participants sit cross-legged on woven floor mats in front of a hand-carved *tanoa* (wooden bowl), which has a long rope decorated with small cowrie shells, and finished off with a larger, white cowrie shell, symbolising the line to the ancestral spirits. Guests offer a bundle of *yaqona* to the hosts in a custom known as *sevusevu*, the name also given to the gift of *yaqona*. The *yaqona* is scraped, cleaned and pounded with a large mortar. This is a laborious, time-consuming process requiring much energy, but it's easier than in pre-European days, when the virgins of the village chewed the *yaqona* to soften it to the right consistency. The pulp is then put into a small cloth sack and mixed with water in the tanoa, where it is kneaded and strained. When it reaches the right consistency (thick and dirty), the person mixing it runs both hands around the rim of the *tanoa*, and claps hollowly three times.

A *bilo* or cup made from a coconut shell sliced in half – in former days it was the upper skull of a defeated enemy – is passed to the guest of honour, who claps once and drinks the concoction in one mouthful. The man sitting next to the person in charge of the *tanoa* now says '*Aah*', and everyone at the ceremony responds with '*Maca*' (pronounced 'ma-tha' and meaning empty). And so it goes on until everyone has participated or until the entire bowl of kava has been consumed.

During the long and intoxicating ritual of the *yaqona* bowl many tense political and community situations have been diffused. There may be slight varia-

Cocktail hour

tions, but the ceremony always involves a certain solemnity, clapping, plenty of drinking, and a calm, relaxed atmosphere.

Other Drinks

Various imported beers are available in Fiji, but be sure to try the nation's own brews. **Fiji Bitter** is a pale lager with a crisp taste, and **Fiji Gold** is a low-calorie beer. Both are brewed in Lautoka and bottled locally by the Fosters Group.

Local brew

Lautoka is also home of South Pacific Distilleries, where **Fiji Golden Rum**, **Booth's Gin**, **Bounty Cossack Vodka** and **Old Club Whisky** are distilled and distributed. The raw material of the rum, molasses, is a by-product of the milling process at the Lautoka Sugar Mill just down the road.

Grapevines are not grown in Fiji, but two brands of wine are made from imported grape juice, Meridan Moselle and Suvanna Moselle. Australian and New Zealand wines feature strongly on most restaurant wine lists.

Bottled water at a reasonable cost is readily available in stores and supermarkets. Aqua Pacific and Fiji Water are both bottled in Fiji. In towns, resorts and hotels, some tap water is all right to drink, but it's wise to ask first. In some places, especially the outer islands, water needs to be boiled before drinking. Soft drinks are available everywhere. Don't expect to buy fresh milk; most of it is long-life or powdered. The best drink in Fiji is milk from the green coconut, sweet and refreshing, and on sale at markets and roadside stalls.

HANDY TRAVEL TIPS

An A–Z Summary of Practical Information

A

ACCOMMODATION (see also YOUTH HOSTELS, and the list of RECOMMENDED HOTELS on pages 128–36)

Every type of accommodation is available in Fiji: bed and breakfasts; home-stays and village-stays in remote places for intrepid travellers; backpacker accommodation for the budget-conscious; 'flashpacker' establishments for those who want the informality of backpacking without roughing it; villas for longer visits; and various hotels and resorts, from mid-range to upmarket, some of which specialise in surfing and diving holidays. You can also charter a boat or an entire island, or indulge in a luxury cruise.

The style of accommodation also varies, ranging from beachfront bungalows, traditional thatched-roof *bures* or single, double and dormitory rooms. Many hotels incorporate Fijian design to intensify the Pacific island atmosphere. Larger hotels are found mainly on Viti Levu and offer a range of services, including restaurants, cafés, bars, pool, gift shops and tourist information desks. Some also have spa and gym facilities. Nearly all hotels and resorts have traditional 'island nights' of Fijian singing and dancing. Most offer free transfer from the airport, so a good option is to book accommodation at least for the first night.

Self-catering homes and villas are ideal for families or groups. There are a number of these around the more populated areas of Taveuni, Savusavu and the Coral Coast.

Backpacker accommodation and village stays (where you lodge with a family in a village) represent excellent value for money for those on a tight budget. Staying with a local family also allows a unique insight into Fijian life.

If you intend travelling to popular locations during the peak season (April to October), booking ahead is a wise move. A comprehensive list of accommodation in Fiji can be found at the Fijian Visitors' Bureau website, <www.bulafiji.com>.

AIRPORTS

Nadi International Airport is situated 9km (5½ miles) north of Nadi town. Nausori International Airport is 23km (14 miles) northeast of downtown Suva. Air Pacific and Qantas flights to and from Sydney arrive and depart from Nausori, but most international flights arrive at Nadi. At both airports, most visitors are transferred to their accommodation by resort or hotel courtesy cars, but there are also plenty of taxis. Domestic airports are located throughout the country, and travel between the two main islands, Viti Levu and Vanua Levu, is by air and sea. Peak season is April to October, and air fares are higher in December–January and April–June. Visitors to Fiji must pay F$30 departure tax; children under 12 are exempt.

The major seaports are Suva (the largest), Lautoka, Levuka and Malau (off Vanua Levu). Lautoka is the main port for western Viti Levu, with facilities for bulk loading of sugar and pine chips.

B

BUDGETING FOR YOUR TRIP

A budget traveller can anticipate spending between F$80 and F$90 per day for food, accommodation and transport. Middle-of-the-road tourists should allow around F$170 a day, less if you're with a friend.

Accommodation. Prices range from F$20 per person per night at backpacker establishments to F$90 per person per night at a mid-range hotel, and from $170 and upwards for top-end accommodation.

Meals and drinks. Having meals at a hotel or resort restaurant may be cheaper or more expensive than eating at a non-resort restaurant, so check carefully before you book. Dinner at a non-resort restaurant costs F$15–$20 per person; a bottle of wine is about F$15 and beer is around $F4 per bottle. If you're self-catering and want to keep costs down, shop for fruit and vegetables at local markets.

Local transport. Boat transfers are sometimes included in the price of accommodation, but are mostly up to the individual, and cost from F$40 for a one-way ticket depending on the destination. If you intend to island-hop, passes are a cheaper option than single tickets. The Yasawa Flyer, connecting islands in the Yasawa Group, has Bula passes at F$199 for seven days' hopping. For coaches, passes on the Feejee Experience begin at F$396 for a four-day pass to F$558 for their Lei Low pass of six days. Fiji Express and Sunset Express run air-conditioned buses between Nadi and Suva and will stop at major hotels along the Queens Road; fares are from F$12 to about F$27. Hiring a car costs about F$120 per day, but shop around for deals.

Activities. Resort guests can expect free cultural experiences, such as kava drinking and *meke*, and outdoor games like volleyball. Some resorts allow free use of kayaks, but most other activities are extra. As a guide, an introductory dive costs F$150, parasailing F$80, water-skiing F$80 and jet-skiing F$80 for 15 minutes. A surfing or diving package makes such activities affordable, and it's worth taking your own mask, fins and snorkel.

C

CAR HIRE

Cars, four-wheel-drive vehicles and vans are available from major car-hire firms such as Avis, Budget and Hertz, and from local agencies such as Aims Rent-A-Car (Nadi; tel: 672 8310) and Trip n' Tours (Savusavu; tel: 885 3154). Rates vary; the longer the hire period, the better the deal. A valid driver's licence is required, with a minimum driver's age of 21 or 25, depending on the company.

CLIMATE

Fiji has a tropical climate, with relatively minor variations in temperature throughout the year. The drier winter months are between May and November, when days are long and fine with cooling southeast trade winds. Average winter temperatures range from a maximum of 26°C (79°F) to a minimum of 20°C (68°F). The wet season (summer) is from December to April, when it's hot and humid. Summer temperatures average between 30°C (86°F) and 25°C (73°F), with cooler temperatures in the upland interior of the larger islands. The following chart gives average temperatures at Suva.

	J	F	M	A	M	J	J	A	S	O	N	D
Max °C	29	29	29	29	28	27	26	26	27	27	28	29
Min °C	23	23	23	23	22	21	20	20	21	21	22	23
Max °F	84	84	84	84	82	81	79	79	81	81	82	84
Min °F	73	73	73	73	72	70	68	68	70	70	72	73

CLOTHING

Dress is casual throughout the islands, and light, loose-fitting clothing works best. Pack T-shirts, shorts, slacks and sandals; for women, take dresses for evenings. A hat protects from the sun's rays. A wrap-around *sulu* (sarong) – worn by Fijian men and women – can be used as a sheet, dress, trousers or blanket. Dress modestly when visiting villages or in town, and save the skimpy gear for beach or pool.

CRIME AND SAFETY

Fiji has one of the world's lowest crime rates, but that's no reason not to take normal precautions. Use safe-deposit boxes at your resort or hotel, and don't leave expensive items on display or unwatched.

In the cities, as everywhere else in the world, there is generally a greater chance of criminal activity. Keep to well-lit streets at night. Police patrol the streets and towns, and are regularly on the prowl with speed detectors.

In Suva, watch out for Fijian men (usually with a canvas package in hand) who greet you with a hearty '*Bula*', ask your name and immediately carve it onto a sword or mask; they then demand that you buy it. In bars, overly sociable people may expect you to buy them drinks.

People of any age may approach you with a clipboard wanting you to donate to some worthy medical cause that will help their dying mother/brother/aunt, etc. Do not be taken in.

Hitchhiking is not recommended.

When swimming or snorkelling, be aware of tidal changes and currents. It's always best to go into the water with someone else.

CUSTOMS AND ENTRY REQUIREMENTS

A four-month entry visa is granted upon arrival to visitors who have both a passport that's valid for at least three months beyond the intended period of stay, and a ticket for return or onward travel to another country. Business-purpose visas are issued for 14 days.

Meat, dairy products, plants, seeds and flowers cannot be brought into Fiji without the necessary licences from the Ministry of Agriculture. The following duty-free items can be brought into the country: 250 cigarettes or 250 grams of tobacco; spirits not exceeding 2.25 litres; wine or beer up to 4.5 litres; and other durable goods not exceeding F$30 per passenger.

For further information, contact Customs, tel: 672 2191 or fax: 672 0557.

D

DRIVING

Road conditions. Fiji has about 3,300km (2,060 miles) of roads, over half of which are sealed. Viti Levu is circled by a 500km (300-mile) road. Most of this is sealed, although some maps show it as fully sealed. On Vanua Levu, the second-largest island, a sealed and scenically spectacular drive runs between Savusavu in the south and Labasa in the north.

Dangers. Wherever you are, watch out for cattle, horses and goats that feed on the edge of the highway and may wander across the road at night, and the occasional deep, wide pothole. Villagers walk along the roads dangerously close to passing vehicles. Groups often gather and sit for a chat close to the road in or near their communities. Watch out for local drivers, who appear to have little road sense and will overtake at the worst possible moments – on blind corners, across double lines and in the face of oncoming cars.

High speed bumps are in place as you enter or leave any village, no matter how small the population, so keep well within speed limits of 20km/h (12mph). Road maps are virtually non-existent, except for those showing city streets. Not all streets are signposted, especially out of town. Parking attendants are diligent in collecting F$20 parking fines. Locals often ask for a ride if you've got room, and giving a lift is a great way to garner local information; it's amazing how many people can squeeze into a car.

Regulations. Drive on the left. Seatbelts are compulsory except for the driver. The maximum speed limit is 50km/h (31mph) in built-up areas and 80km/h (50mph) on highways.

Fuel. Petrol stations are located throughout Fiji, but are less frequently encountered in rural areas. Credit cards are not generally accepted in payment for fuel.

E

ELECTRICITY

Electrical current in Fiji is 240 volts AC 50Hz. Fiji has three-pin power outlets identical to those used in Australia and New Zealand. The leading hotels and resorts offer universal outlets for 240V or 110V shavers, hairdryers, etc. Carry your own adaptor if necessary.

EMBASSIES AND HIGH COMMISSIONS

All embassies are located in Suva.
Australia: 37 Prices Road, Tamavua, tel: 338 2211.
New Zealand: 10th Floor, Reserve Bank Building, Pratt Street, tel: 331 1422.
UK: Victoria House, 47 Gladstone Road, tel: 322 9100.
USA: 31 Loftus Street, tel: 331 4466.

EMERGENCIES

If you have an emergency while staying at a resort, visitors are advised to dial 0 to get initial help from the resort office. Resorts on outer islands are equipped to handle fire and medical emergencies.

Outside of resorts contact:
Police and Ambulance **911**
Fire **917**
Fiji Recompression Chamber **336 2172**

G

GAY AND LESBIAN TRAVELLERS

Homosexuality has not been legalised, and although communities appear to tolerate openly gay couples, displays of affection in public are considered offensive. Generally, gays seem to be accepted, although there are no bars or nightclubs specifically for them.

GETTING TO FIJI

Fiji is the central stopover in the South Pacific, so there are plenty of flight options. Shop around for the best deals. April to October is the main holiday season, but the period between December and the middle of January is the busiest time of year to travel as it is the Christmas school holiday period in New Zealand and Australia, and both international and local flights can be booked out months in advance.

From North America. Air New Zealand (a Star Alliance member) and Air Fiji (Fiji's national airline) have flights from North America. Both airlines have multiple weekly flights departing from Los Angeles and arriving at Nadi International Airport. Air Pacific also operates three direct flights a week between Fiji and Los Angeles and two flights a week from Vancouver via Hawaii. Flight time from Los Angeles is 10 hours 20 minutes, and most international flights arrive before dawn. Flights on Fiji's domestic airlines, Pacific Sun and Air Fiji, transfer passengers to outer islands within a few hours of landing.

From Japan. Air Pacific flies direct from Tokyo twice a week.

From Australia. Air New Zealand, Qantas and Air Pacific offer direct flights from Brisbane, Sydney and Melbourne. Watch out for special deals.

From New Zealand. Air New Zealand and Air Pacific schedule daily direct three-hour flights from Auckland and Christchurch.

From Europe. Air New Zealand offers a daily service from London via Los Angeles either direct to Fiji or stopping en route either in New Zealand or Australia. Direct flying time is about 23 hours. (From Asia 12 hours; from Hawaii seven hours.)

GUIDES AND TOURS

Package holidays are popular, and many tourists stay in just one or two locations. For those who want to venture away from their resort, taking an organised tour is a good idea, especially because signage on roads is poor, making independent travel difficult. Most resorts have their own travel desk with racks of brochures detailing everything from half-day to multi-day tours. Many tours work to a theme or specific activity, such as eco-tours, city sights, nightlife, cruises, biking and hiking, and village visits.

On a boat tour you can visit a number of island locations in a single day, and four-wheel-drive tours allow access to highland areas. Use exhilarating rafting and kayaking trips to explore hidden rivers and gorges with local guides. Prices vary according to duration and type, but day tours on average are from F$60 to F$150 per person.

Tours from Nadi focus mostly on island-hopping around the offshore islands or visiting villages. Most day tours depart at 9am and return at 5pm, with some half-day tours returning at 3pm. Aerial sightseeing by helicopter or seaplane is a spectacular option (for more information, see <www.fijiseaplanes.com>).

Family-orientated tours based around the Coral Coast include riding on the Coral Coast Railroad to Natadola, Kula Eco Park and the Korolevu Cultural Centre.

H

HEALTH AND MEDICAL CARE

Fiji is free from rabies, malaria and other major diseases that are endemic to most tropical countries. Yellow fever and cholera vaccinations are required if coming from an infected area as designated by the World Health Organisation.

Cuts and scratches become quickly infected in the tropics, so pay immediate attention to even the smallest cut. The sun is intense, and pale skins will burn quickly – wear a hat and shirt, and apply a sunscreen. Drink water frequently – it's easy to become dehydrated.

Travel insurance is advisable, as medical services are limited and hospitals are good but underfunded, though capable of handling basic emergencies. In extreme cases, patients are evacuated by air to Australia or New Zealand.

Hospitals and medical centres. Hospitals are located in the major towns and cities, and health centres in rural areas. Hotels and resorts keep a qualified nurse on the premises and a doctor on call. Surgery hours are usually between 8.30am and 5pm. Suva's Private Hospital is modern and equipped to handle overseas patients with medical insurance cover. It has two operating theatres, a medical centre and a 24-hour emergency unit. At government-run hospitals like the CWM in Suva, there is a modest charge for patients who are not Fijian citizens.

Chemists. Chemists are open during normal shopping hours. Doctors and chemists are listed in the Fiji Yellow Pages.

HOLIDAYS

Major public holidays include:

New Year's Day	**1 January**
National Youth Day	**Early March**
Easter	**March/April**
Ratu Sakuna Day	**Around 29 May**
Queen's Birthday	**Around 14 June**
Constitution Day	**Around 27 July**
Birth of Lord Krishna	**August/September**
Prophet Mohammed's Birthday	**Between July and December**
Fiji Day/Independence Day	**Early October**
Christmas Day	**25 December**
Boxing Day	**26 December**

L

LANGUAGE

Fijian and English are both spoken, but English is recognised as the official language. *'Bula'* (pronounced 'm boo-lah'), Fiji's official greeting, is the word you hear and use most frequently. A common phrase typifying the happy nature of Fijians is *'Sega na leqa'* (pronounced 'seng-gah-na-leng-gah'), meaning 'no worries'.

In Fijian, vowels are pronounced the same as in English, but some consonants change. B is 'mb' as in bamboo. C is 'th' as in that. D is 'nd' as in candy. J is 'ch' as in church. G is 'ng' as in singing. Q is 'ng' as in angry. Here is a list of commonly used words and phrases.

English	Fijian	Pronunciation
hello	**bula**	'*m boo-lah*'
good morning	**nis sa yadra**	'*ni sah yarn drah*'
goodbye (informal)	**moce**	'*mow-they*'
please	**kerekere**	'*cayray-cayray*'
thank you/good	**vinaka**	'*vee-nakha*'
excuse me	**tulou**	'*too low*'
yes	**lo**	'*ee-oh*'
no	**sega**	'*seng-gah*'
eat	**kana**	'*kah-nah*'
woman	**marama**	'*mmah-raam-mah*'
man	**turaga**	'*too-ran-gah*'
child	**gone**	'*ngo-ne*'
church	**vale ni lotu**	'*vah-ley nee low-too*'
shop/store	**sitoa**	'*see-tah-ah*'
earth oven	**lovo**	'*low-voh*'
sarong	**sulo**	'*sue-loo*'
house	**bure**	'*mboo-ree*'
toilet	**ale lailai**	'*vale lie lie*'

M

MAPS

Good maps of Fiji are virtually non-existent. You can buy city street maps from main post offices, but don't expect to find comprehensive road maps if you intend hiring a car and driving yourself around.

MEDIA

Fiji's media includes free-to-air and pay television, 12 radio stations, three daily English newspapers, three weekly vernacular newspapers, and news and business magazines. The main English-language daily newspaper is the *Fiji Times*.

MONEY

Currency. Fijian Dollar (FJD; symbol F$) = 100 cents. Notes are in denominations of F$50, 20, 10, 5 and 2. Coins are in denominations of F$1, and 50, 20, 10, 5, 2 and 1 cents. It's a good idea to carry plenty of small change, including notes, because taxis and buses rarely have change. Small amounts are also more convenient when purchasing market items.

Currency exchange. Currency-exchange facilities are available at airports, trading banks and most hotels. You get better exchange rates by using a credit card or an automatic teller machine (ATM) than from the banks. ANZ Bank has a 24-hour currency-exchange service at Nadi International Airport.

Credit cards. Most establishments accept credit and debit cards, American Express, Diners Club, MasterCard and Visa.

Traveller's cheques. Traveller's cheques (preferably in Australian dollars or pounds sterling) are readily cashed in any Fiji bank, most hotels, and duty-free shops. Most transactions include 12.5 percent value added tax (VAT).

ATMs. Cash machines can be found in Nadi, Suva, Lautoka and Sigatoka. They may not accept foreign credit cards.

Banks. There are branches of the ANZ, Westpac and Colonial National banks in the major urban areas.

O

OPENING HOURS

Banks are open Monday–Thursday 10am–3pm, Friday to 4pm. Government and business offices are open five days a week, usually 8am–4.30pm (Friday to 4pm) with at least an hour for lunch between 1pm and 2pm. Most shops and other commercial outlets are open five days a week, Monday–Thursday 8am–5pm, Friday to 6pm. Saturday business hours are 8am–1pm. A few businesses open on Sundays and public holidays, including service stations and pharmacies, but don't expect much else. City post offices are open Monday–Friday 8am–4.30pm; in towns they close half an hour earlier. Be aware of 'Fiji Time' – the rather casual attitude Fijians have about being in the right place at the right time.

P

POLICE

Fiji is still a relatively safe country in which to travel. Statistics show a 3 percent decrease in crime in 2007. On the roads, watch out for police with hand-held speed detectors. If you should become a victim of crime, report the details to the police immediately and insist on either a copy of the report or reference number for your insurance purposes. The police emergency number is 911.

POST OFFICES

Post Fiji operates the country's postal services. Posting a letter within the country costs 18 cents, international postcards 27 cents, and international letters up to 30 grams, 31 cents. Mail is held for up to two months poste restante. For more information on Post Fiji's services, see <www.postfiji.com.fj>. Post offices are located in all major cities and towns. Opening hours in cities are Monday–Friday 8am–4.30pm, closing at 4pm in towns.

R

RELIGION

Fiji is a melting pot of the world's great religions – churches, mosques and temples can be found throughout the country. All faiths appear to practise tolerance of each other. Surveys indicate that almost all of Fiji's inhabitants belong to some kind of organised religion: 47 percent Christian, 40 percent Hindu and 8 percent Muslim. The majority of Christian Fijians are Methodists. Visitors are welcome at Sunday worship throughout the country.

Suva has both a Catholic and Anglican cathedral, and Nadi boasts a Hindu temple, two mosques and various churches.

T

TELEPHONE

Local telephone services, including paging and voice-mail, are provided by Telecom Fiji Limited, while Fiji International Telecommunications Ltd (FINTEL) is responsible for international services, including international and domestic direct dialling, telex and facsimile. Mobile communications are available from Vodafone Fiji; the outer islands are connected by radio telephone. Over 1,500 public phone booths *(drua)* can be used with a Tele-Card. You can purchase these cards in denominations of F$50, F$20, F$10, F$5 and F$3 from post offices and service stations.

To make a call within Fiji, simply dial the local number. For international calls, dial 00, followed by the country code, area code and telephone number. The international country code for Fiji is 679, and there are no area codes. Most hotels have direct-dialling facilities.

Those wishing to use a mobile phone in Fiji should arrange roaming with your service provider before leaving home. Vodafone gives excellent coverage in most locations.

TIME ZONES

Fiji is 12 hours ahead of Greenwich Mean Time (GMT).

London	New York	**Suva**	Auckland	Sydney
9pm	4pm	**9am**	9am	7am

TIPPING

Tipping is not encouraged in Fiji, and a gratuity is up to the individual. In lieu of daily tipping, some resorts operate a staff Christmas fund where gratuities are shared.

TOILETS

It's always a good idea to carry tissues and a liquid hand-sanitiser. Most toilets are flush, with some composting toilets in operation that seem to do the job effectively. In remote areas, you might find the occasional long drop and coconut husks for toilet paper.

TOURIST INFORMATION

The Fiji Visitors' Bureau has two offices: in Suva (corner of Thomson and Scott streets, tel: 330 2433), and at Nadi International Airport (Arrivals Concourse, tel: 672 2433); see also <www.bulafiji.com>. Most resorts also have racks of tourist brochures. Be wary of unauthorised information booths in the main towns, which are generally a ploy to get you into specific accommodation or involved in some investment scheme.

TRANSPORT

Planes. Air Pacific, Qantas and Air New Zealand operate regular services from Australia, New Zealand, Rarotonga, Japan and the USA, landing at Nadi International Airport, and all major islands and island groups are linked by air or sea transport. Nausori Airport, 20km (12 miles) from Suva, also operates regular services to most airstrips.

Domestic airlines Pacific Sun and Air Fiji provide domestic flights to smaller airports within the country.

Passengers are advised to keep luggage within the recommended weight and size limitations and be prepared for delays in arrivals and departures. If you're carrying large items, such as surfboards or mountain bikes, check requirements when you buy your ticket. Ask Air Fiji about any current domestic air-pass deals. There is no airport shuttle bus from any of the airports. Most hotels arrange complimentary transfers for their guests. A taxi from Nadi Airport to Nadi town costs F$10; the bus costs $F0.80.

Seaplanes and helicopters. Charter seaplanes (<www.turtleair ways.com> or <www.fijiseaplanes.com>) and helicopters (<www. helicopters.com.fj>) operate from Nadi, and are generally used for sightseeing or to access exclusive resorts.

Buses. Local buses with open windows provide a regular, cheap service highly recommended to those who like a close encounter with friendly locals. Wave them down and stop wherever you need to. Express buses stop and depart from designated terminals and bus shelters. Air-conditioned coaches run between Nadi and Suva along the Coral Coast on Viti Levu twice daily and will pick up and drop off at hotels and resorts. This trip is approximately three hours by express bus or four to five hours by local bus.

The Feejee Experience company offers flexible travel passes for independent travellers on Viti Levu, allowing them the freedom to spend as long as they want at each destination. Different types of pass are available – the Hula Loop pass is recommended for a minimum trip of six days, Lei Low for eight days or more. Some passes include accommodation, as well as bus travel. For more information, contact Feejee Experience, Aerotown Mall, Nadi Airport, tel: 672 3311 or 672 5950; email: <enquiries@feejeeexperience.com>; <www.feejeeexperience.com>.

'Fiji Time' – the tendency of Fijians not to be punctual – doesn't always apply to bus schedules and other forms of public transport: be on time, just in case.

Ferries. Ferries and fast catamarans depart regularly from Denarau, near Nadi, servicing the Mamanuca and Yasawa islands. There are numerous carriers, some specific to tourist accommodation. South Sea Cruises (<www.ssc.com.fj>) covers most of the Mamanuca islands, and Awesome Adventures (<www.awesomefiji.com>) runs the Yasawa Flyer, connecting islands in the Yasawa Group.

Regular ferry services also depart from Suva to Vanua Levu and Kadavu. Beachcomber Cruises, Patterson Brothers and Consort Shipping carry passengers and vehicles. Trips can be long and unpleasant in rough conditions.

Cars, bicycles and taxis. For information about driving in Fiji, see DRIVING *(page 113)*. Hiring scooters and bikes can be fun for local excursions, but these vehicles are not recommended for long journeys. Some car hire firms hire scooters *(see page 111)*, as does Trip n' Tours in Savusavu (tel: 885 3154; fax: 885 3174).

Taxis are plentiful, but negotiate the price prior to your journey and make sure you have change. Taxis wait at stands or can be waved down in the street.

TRAVELLERS WITH DISABILITIES

With many public buildings, libraries, toilets and theatres yet to become disability-friendly, and few ramps or lifts, Fiji is not well suited to the disabled traveller. The streets are often rough, with few ramps for crossing the road. Getting on and off public buses will be a problem for people with walking difficulties. There are wheelchairs at airports, and the Savusavu Rotary Club has a project underway to equip disabled locals with wheelchairs, so maybe things will improve.

At many resorts the sandy paths, which have numerous steps, create problems for wheelchair-users. Some resorts have guest rooms specifically designed for the disabled; check before booking. To find out which resorts have accommodation suitable for the disabled, as well as information about assistance with transport, contact the Fiji Disabled People's Association (355 Waimanu Road, Suva; tel: 331 203).

W

WATER

Fresh water reticulated in Nadi, Suva, Lautoka and other major towns has been treated and is generally safe to drink. Bottled water is available, including two Fiji-bottled brands, Aqua Pacific and Fiji Water.

WEBSITES AND INTERNET SERVICES

The Fiji Islands Visitors' Bureau website is at <www.bulafiji.com>. There are a number of other useful websites giving information for people intending to visit Fiji:

Island sites
<www.savusavufiji.com> – Savusavu and Vanua Levu
<www.levukafiji.com> – Lomaiviti Group
<www.fijibudget.com> – Yasawa islands (budget resorts)

Other sites
<www.airfiji.com.fj> – Air Fiji
<www.pacificsun.com.fj> – Pacific Sun
<www.fijiseaplanes.com> – seaplanes
<www.met.gov.fj> – Fiji weather service
<www.ats.com.fj> – Fiji flight schedules
<www.ftib.org.fj> – Fiji Islands Trade and Investment Bureau
<www.fiji.islands-holiday.com/travel.html> – general information

<www.fiji-island.com> – general information
<www.fijibure.com> – the village-stay experience
<www.fijiatoz.com/t.html> – Fiji A to Z

A number of small, dark and suffocatingly hot Internet cafés exist in the towns and cities. Prices range from F$1 to F$2 per half-hour. Most hotels and resorts are also equipped with Internet services, but prices are higher, sometimes as much as F$1 per minute. Private I-Surf Prepaid Internet Kiosks are available at Nadi International Airport, and users can purchase prepaid Internet access cards from selected outlets around the airport complex.

WEIGHTS AND MEASURES

Fiji uses the metric system.

Y

YOUTH HOSTELS

Membership of the Youth Hostel Association is not essential to stay in a youth hostel, but it does entitle you to cheaper rates and travel discounts. There are 42 youth hostels in a wide variety of locations, including offshore islands – Beachcomber, Yanuca (surfing), Yasawas and Mana – and mainland locations – Pacific Harbour, Nadi, Suva and Sigatoka. Hostelling is a great way to meet other budget travellers.

A number of factors influence price options: type of accommodation (single, double, dormitory; separate bungalows or *bures*); whether rooms are fan-cooled or air-conditioned; bathrooms shared or en suite. Some accommodation includes home cooking; in others (particularly island locations) the all-inclusive price covers meals and activities. Prices average around F$30 per person per night, but some are as low as F$12. Phones, faxes and Internet facilities are on hand, and most hostels are child- and wheelchair-friendly. A full range of Fiji's youth hostels can be found at <www.trav.com/hostels/fiji>.

Recommended Hotels

Most accommodation is *bure*-style (a thatched-roof cottage) or incorporates traditional Fijian design. All resort premises offer a wide range of accommodation, from private rooms to dorms to separate bungalows. You'd be unlucky to find one without a pool or restaurant.

When choosing accommodation, factor in the cost of airport transfers – particularly if you are staying on an offshore island – meals and activities such as snorkelling and kayaking. Backpacker dorm beds cost from F$20 without meals to F$50 including meals. A standard resort in Nadi will cost from F$100 a night, but on islands expect to pay at least F$200. Luxury resorts start from about F$400 per night and can be as much as F$1,100 plus. Walk-in rates are available from February to March, but it's wiser to book your first few nights. You need to reserve accommodation on remote islands, as most involve sea transfers.

The following price guide gives an indication of starting prices per night for a room for two. These can sometimes vary by F$100 or F$200 depending on individual requirements.

$$$$$	above F$400
$$$$	F$250–400
$$$	F$100–250
$$	F$50–100
$	Below F$50

VITI LEVU

NADI

First Landing Resort $$$$ *Vuda Point, tel: 666 6171, fax: 666 8882, <www.firstlandingresort.com>.* According to local legend, the first people to reach Fiji arrived here around 1500BC. Set in a tropical garden beside Nadi's only white-sand beach, it's a popular land base for yachtsmen arriving at nearby Vuda Point Marina.

Nadi is about 30 minutes away, and it's a 15-minute drive in either direction to Nadi Airport or Lautoka.

Heaven's Edge $ *PO Box 40, Sabeto.* This backpacker establishment is perched on the edge of a mountain in the highlands one and a half hours' drive from Nadi, and aptly named for its stunning, nearly 360-degree panoramic view. Communal dining room, bathroom and toilet facilities, with some more private *bures* available. It's a great place to meet and talk to Fijians. Activities include hiking, horse-riding, birdwatching and pig-hunting. Meals are included. *Rates are per person.* Book through agencies.

Mercure Accor Hotel Nadi $$$ *Queens Road, Martintar, Nadi, tel: 672 2255, fax: 672 0187, <www.accorhotels.com.fj>.* Formerly called the Grand Melanesian, this hotel has expansive grounds and a fabulous pool setting with alfresco restaurant extending to the edge. Five minutes from the airport and 10 minutes from downtown Nadi.

Nadi Bay Hotel $–$$$ *Wailoaloa Road, Martinar, Nadi, tel: 672 3599, fax: 672 0092, <www.fijinadibayhotel.com>.* The hotel offers a variety of accommodation, from dorms to rooms to air-conditioned apartments; choose from fans or air-conditioning, shared or single occupancy. Conveniently located a 10-minute drive from the airport. The social scene attracts a young to middle-aged clientele. Excellent restaurant, plus bars, pool and laundry service.

Nadi Holiday Inn Backpackers Youth Hostel $ *Cawa Road, Martintar, Nadi, tel: 672 2158, fax: 670 1541, <www.fijihostels. com>.* Open 24 hours. Towels and linen provided. Rates vary according to whether the room is shared or private, or if there's a fan or air-conditioning. Breakfast included. *Rates are per person.*

CORAL COAST

Beqa Lagoon Resort $$$$ *PO Box 112, Deuba, tel: 330 4042, fax: 330 4028, <www.beqalagoonresort.com>.* Beqa Island, 7.5km (5 miles) off the coast of Viti Levu, 130km (81 miles) from Nadi, is tiny, covering only 15 sq km (6 sq miles). It has no towns, no roads and only a few isolated villages. Popular with visitors, especially fishermen and divers, Beqa is the home of the Pipeline and Frigate Passage surfing sites, and there are several dive sites. Choose from a private beachfront *bure* with equally private plunge pool, or a larger, family-size *bure*. Great restaurant, with regular live music, *meke* and firewalking displays at night. Meal plans available.

Hideaway Resort $$$$ *PO Box 233, Sigatoka; tel: 650 0177, fax: 652 0025, <www.hideawayfiji.com>*. Single-level villas, colourful, spacious and luxurious, are sited on a beach 20km (12½ miles) east of Sigatoka. With a swimming pool, gymnasium and PADI dive school, there's plenty to do. You can also surf in front of the resort, kayak, windsurf or play golf nearby. There's a great restaurant, which stages cultural shows and regular entertainment. Children are catered for.

Mango Bay Resort $–$$$ *PO Box 1720, Sigatoka, tel: 653 0069, fax: 653 0138, <www.mangobayresortfiji.com>*. This was Fiji's first flashpacker establishment, and everyone's still talking about its young, fun atmosphere. Accommodation ranges from group dorms and safari tents to beachfront *bures*. All manner of watersports are available in a simply stunning setting.

Pacific Pearl Hotel $$$–$$$$ *Queens Road, Deuba, tel: 345 0022, fax: 345 0262, <www.thepearlsouthpacific.com>*. The Pearl is located on the beachfront near Pacific Harbour between Suva and Nadi, with a winding river running through the property. The guest rooms are luxurious. In the public rooms, comfortable couches, ottomans and coffee tables are arranged so that guests can relax and enjoy the views. Choose where to dine: the sophisticated Mantarae Restaurant, alfresco Beach Bar and BBQ, or the casual Bistro, by the pool. To top it all, the property is home to the Greens South Pacific, an 18-hole, 72-par championship golf course designed by Robert Trent Jones Jr.

Vatulele Island Resort $$$$$ *Vatulele Island, tel: 672 0300, fax: 672 0062, <www.vatulele.com>*. Vatulele Island is located 32km (20 miles) off the Coral Coast. The resort has 19 spacious and luxurious *bures* decorated in traditional Fijian style, set in front of a sugar-white sand beach. Access to the island is by plane. The resort has its own PADI diving facility. As well as accommodation, the price includes gourmet meals, alcohol and most activities, excluding scuba diving and game-fishing.

SUVA

Homestay Suva $$$ *265 Princes Road, Tamavua Heights, Suva, tel: 337 0395, fax: 337 0947, email: <homestaysuva@connect.com.fj>.* This colonial mansion, five minutes' drive from downtown Suva, has been transformed into a B&B with clean, airy rooms. It's a comfortable and friendly place. The deck has wonderful views of the harbour.

Nanette's Homestay $$$ *56 Extension Street, Suva, tel: 331 6316, fax: 331 6902, email: <nanettes@connect.com.fj>.* A friendly B&B near the hospital, a 20-minute walk into downtown Suva. The upstairs rooms are of varying sizes, and there's communal TV lounge and kitchen. Downstairs are three self-contained apartments.

Rainforest Lodge $–$$ *Princes Road, Colo-i-Suva, Suva, tel: 332 0562, fax: 332 0113, <www.raintreelodge.com>.* Wake to the sound of birdsong at this superior backpacker establishment 11km (7 miles) from downtown Suva at the entrance to Colo-i-Suva Forest Park. Accommodation options include dorms, individual rooms with shared or private bathroom, and comparatively luxurious bungalows with TV, refrigerator and bath.

Suva Apartments $$ *17 Bau Street, Suva, tel: 330 4280.* Suva Apartments' concrete block units are clean, modern and well equipped. A great option for longer stays in the city. Very popular, so book well in advance.

Tanoa Plaza Hotel $$$–$$$$ *Corner of Gordon and Malcolm streets, Suva, tel: 331 4233, fax: 330 1300, <www.tanoahotels.com>.* Great upmarket accommodation on a hillside location with stunning views, and within easy walking distance of Suva's shops, markets and restaurants. The Tanoa Plaza has a tour desk, swimming pool, bars and a good selection of restaurants.

SUNSHINE COAST

Beetham's Beach Cottages $–$$ *Nananu-i-Ra Island, PO Box 5, Rakiraki, tel/fax: 669 4132, <www.bethams.com.fj>*. Beetham's runs a small boat to take visitors on the 10-minute ride from Ellington Wharf to Nananu-i-Ra Island, 4km (2½ miles) off the north coast of Viti Levu. You can safely leave your car at Ellington Wharf for a small charge. The cottages are cosy, self-contained units, great for groups or families, with a low-key, friendly and relaxed atmosphere. You can eat at the restaurant or cater for yourself, using provisions from the resort's shop.

Wananavu Beach Resort $$$$ *PO Box 305, Rakiraki, tel: 669 4433, fax: 669 4499, <www.wananavu.com>*. The resort is sited on a headland near Rakiraki, overlooking the sea and Nananu-i-Ra Island. The absence of phones, radios or TVs in the *bures* ensures that you leave the modern world behind. Most activities are water-based – there's snorkelling directly offshore and excellent diving nearby. Special dive and accommodation packages are available, as well as meal plans.

MAMANUCA AND YASAWA GROUPS

MAMANUCAS

Beachcomber Island Resort $$–$$$ *Beachcomber Island, tel: 666 2600 (island) or 666 1500 (Lautoka office), fax: 666 4496, <www.beachcomberfiji.com>*. Often referred to as 'Party Island', Beachcomber attracts a young and young-at-heart clientele and specialises in fantastic beach parties and feasts with live music and entertainment. There's a huge range of watersports and a lively, casual atmosphere. Choose from several styles of accommodation, from dormitory to beachfront *bure*. Rates include all meals, but transfers are extra, as are activities other than snorkelling.

Castaway Island Resort $$$$–$$$$$ *Castaway Island, Private Mailbag, Nadi Airport, tel: 666 1233, fax: 666 5753, <www.castawayisland.com>*. A family resort on a 70-hectare (174-acre) island,

Castaway has 66 *bures*, indoor and outdoor restaurants, tennis court and swimming pool. All watersports equipment is available free of charge. There are 20 dive sites within 20 minutes of the island, so make full use of the PADI dive facilities.

YASAWAS

Nanuya Island Resort $$$–$$$$ *Nanuya Lailai, tel: 666 1462 or 666 7633, fax: 666 1462, <www.nanuyafiji.com>*. Four de luxe villas and four quaint traditional *bures* nestle on the hillside overlooking the sea. Prices don't include food, but the restaurant has a fine menu. Transfers are by 30-minute seaplane flight or high-speed catamaran. Scuba diving, kayaking, fly-fishing and village visits can be arranged.

Octopus Resort $$–$$$ *Waya Island, PO Box 1861, Lautoka, tel: 666 6442 (island), fax: 666 6210, <www.octopusresort.com>*. The resort fronts a white-sand beach on Waya Island. Accommodation is as simple as a tent site or can be a chic *bure* with private bathroom, solar-powered hot-water system and open-roofed shower. The resort has its own dive facilities where guests can register for open-water diving courses. Transfers not included in price.

Turtle Island Resort $$$$$ *Nanuya Levu, tel: 800-255-4347 (North America), 0800 285938 (UK), 03 9823 8300 (Australia), <www.turtlefiji.com>*. A stone's throw from Nanuya Lailai is the privately owned Nanuya Levu, site of the luxurious Turtle Island Resort. Accommodation is in one of 14 elegant two-room *bures* facing a gorgeous lagoon. All meals, drinks and activities – including diving, snorkelling, sailing and kayaking – are included in the price, although seaplane transfers are not. Minimum stay of six nights.

SAVUSAVU

Bayside Backpackers $ *37 Lesiaceva Road, Savusavu, tel: 885 3154, email: <tripntour@connect.com.fj>*. Bayside is about 3km (2 miles) from Savusavu (a five-minute drive or half-hour walk).

Accommodation is bedsitter-style, with linen and towels supplied. A black-sand beach is good for swimming, and there's kayaking at high tide or snorkelling along the reef edge at low tide. Snorkelling equipment and surf skis are available free of charge. *Rates are per person.*

La Dolce Vita Holiday Villas $$$$$ *Hibiscus Coast Road, Savusavu, tel: 851 8023, <www.ladolcevitafiji.com>.* The exquisite octagonal-shaped *bures*, which blend beautifully into the small bay setting, follow traditional Fijian design, but are built in contemporary style with concertina glass doors and stainless-steel balcony rails. Fantastic bush walks on the property lead to spectacular vistas across Nekawa Bay. Rates include meals and most activities.

The Hidden Paradise Guest House $ *Main Street, Savusavu, tel: 885 0106, fax: 885 0344.* This atmospheric guesthouse is situated behind the Seaview Café on Savusavu's main road in a handy location. The rooms are fairly basic, and guests share bathroom facilities. Attached to the guesthouse is an excellent café/restaurant offering well-priced Indian, Fijian and European meals. Room charges include breakfast. *Rates are per person.*

Moody's Namena $$$$$ *Namenalala Island, tel: 881 3764, fax: 881 2366, <www.moodysnamenafiji.com>.* Situated in splendid isolation 40km (25 miles) from Savusavu, the island has six private *bures* in spectacular settings overlooking the sea. The owners have done much to preserve the island's natural environment, and there are excellent beaches and bushwalks. Bird life is unsurpassed. Within the Namena Marine Reserve, Moody's has some of Fiji's best reef diving. Stone remains of the Lapita people can be found on one of the island's high points. Minimum stay of five nights. Price includes transfers, meals and use of all equipment, but diving is extra. Closed March and April.

Tropic Splendor $$ *PO Box 306, Savusavu, tel/fax: 851 0152, <www.tropicsplendor.com>.* Only 20 minutes' drive from Savusavu town centre, this beachfront resort is special. Exclusive, reclusive and affordable – a self-contained tropical retreat for travellers who want solitude. Tasteful, traditional-style bungalows are set in flourishing gardens complete with waterlily ponds. The owners live nearby and will assist with any requirements, or leave you completely in peace. You can cook your own meals, or have them cooked for you. Wedding arrangements can also be made.

TAVEUNI

Bibi's Hideaway $–$$ *Matei Road, Taveuni, tel: 888 0443.* Situated an easy 10-minute walk from Matei airstrip, Bibi's offers upmarket backpacker accommodation ranging from dormitories to a small bungalow with two bedrooms and a kitchen for self-catering. Guests are invited to help themselves to fruit from trees in the expansive grounds, and there's a beach close by. *Rates are per person.*

Coconut Grove Beachfront Cottages $$$ *9 Matei Road, Taveuni, tel: 888 0328, fax: 888 2328, <www.coconutgrovefiji.com>.* A small, intimate resort of three traditional-style *bures* equipped with ceiling fans and outdoor lava-rock showers. Cosy, friendly, informal and delightfully welcoming. Excellent swimming, kayaking and snorkelling at low tide from the sandy beach directly in front of the cottages. There's a good restaurant, as well as kava and a Fijian musical group on selected nights. Coconut Grove has a community spirit, and you'll feel part of a big family.

Garden Island Resort $$$ *PO Box 1, Waiyevo, Taveuni, tel: 888 0286, fax: 888 0288, <www.aquatrek.com>.* Sited on the ocean front, the resort overlooks the Somosomo Strait, location of Taveuni's most famous dives. Special accommodation/dive packages are available in conjunction with the resort's professional dive operation, Aqua-Trek. Nitrox facilities are available.

Taveuni Palms $$$$$ *Matei Road, Taveuni, tel: 888 0032, <www.taveunipalmsfiji.com>.* Immaculately maintained five-star property with just two luxurious *bures*. The resort focuses entirely on each guest's privacy and desires, with your own chef, boat and captain, dive master, double kayak, complimentary scuba lessons and private beach. You name it, you've got it. When possible, all meals use ingredients grown in the resort's organic garden.

KADAVU

Dive Kadavu Resort $$$$ *Kadavu Island, tel: 333 7780, fax: 333 7680, <www.divekadavu.com>.* As its name suggests, Dive Kadavu is pitched firmly at the diving fraternity, but there are plenty of other activities on offer, including kayaking, birdwatching and hiking. Accommodation is in *bures*, eight close to the shore and two set back. All are comfortable and well equipped. Transfers are organised from the island's airport by boat to the resort. Rates include transfers and meals.

OVALAU

Bobo's Farm $ *PO Box 149, Levuka, tel: 344 0166, fax: 344 0633, <www.owlfiji.com/bobosfarm.htm>.* This backpacker, farm-stay retreat is situated in a lush valley on the northwest side of Ovalau in the Rukuruku Valley, and is only a 10-minute walk from the sea. The sole guesthouse has two bedrooms, a bathroom and a kitchen. Meals are available on request. Bobo's Farm is run by a local family, and staying here is a good way to get an authentic taste of the Fijian rural way of life. *Rates are per person.*

The Royal Hotel $–$$ *Beach Street, tel: 344 0024, fax: 344 0174, <www.royallevuka.com>.* Built in the 1850s on the waterfront, this is the oldest continuously run hotel in the South Pacific, and is loaded with history and atmosphere. It has a traditional balcony facing the cliffs, polished brass shell casings for ashtrays, a supposedly haunted room and a century-old billiard table. Staying here fits with the whole historic Levuka theme. The dining room serves breakfasts and light snacks, but other meals are best organised in town.

LAU GROUP

Moana's Guest House $$ *PO Box 11, Lomaloma, Vanua Balavu, tel: 889 5006, <www.moanasguesthouses.com>.* Near Sawana on Vanua Balavu, Moana's offers basic but comfortable accommodation, and the price includes meals. Trips can be organised if guests want to experience something more than village life. *Rates are per person.*

Recommended Restaurants

Fiji's climate results in an abundant and continual supply of good fresh fruit and vegetables, adding colour, taste and decoration to even the simplest meal. Seafood is in good supply and often caught and cooked within hours. Crabs, lobster and fresh fish appear on most menus.

In main towns you'll find a range of eateries, from cheap cafés and small, atmospheric restaurants to upmarket restaurants that pride themselves on serving international cuisine. Depending on the style, nearly all offer entrées, mains and desserts. Hotel breakfasts are continental or buffet.

Whether you fancy *kokoda* or curry, fish and chips or chop suey, you're bound to find it in one of the larger towns; Nadi even has a McDonald's if you're desperate. On outer islands it's likely that the only restaurants are those at your accommodation.

The price guidelines below are based on an average main course per person, without wine.

$$$$	above F$40
$$$	F$20–40
$$	F$10–20
$	Below F$10

VITI LEVU

NADI

The Bounty Restaurant and Bar $–$$ *Queens Road, Martinar, Nadi, tel: 672 0840, email: <thebounty@connect.com.fj>*. Large air-conditioned eatery serving a range of well-priced Indian, Chinese and international-style meals, including curries, steaks, pasta, fish and chips, and lobster. Appeals to locals, expatriates and tourists alike. Open daily 9am until late.

Curry House $ *Hospital Road, Nadi, tel: 670 0798.* A popular joint with excellent choice of curries, plus other dishes. Eat indoors or out.

Nano's Nadi $$ *7 Sagayam Road, Nadi, tel: 670 6866.* A colourful Mexican-style eatery with typical spicy dishes, quick service and a friendly atmosphere.

Ports O'Call $$$$ *Denarau Island, Nadi, tel: 675 0777.* This is the Sheraton Fiji Resort's five-star restaurant. In keeping with its 1930s ocean-liner décor, Port O'Call serves food from the cuisines of the world's most famous ports.

CORAL COAST

Oasis Village $–$$ *Arts Village, Pacific Harbour, tel: 345 0617.* Relax with a casual lunch or takeaway of sandwiches, curries and burgers, or stay for dinner and order something more substantial.

Pearl South Pacific $$–$$$$ *Queens Road, Pacific Harbour, tel: 345 0022.* Choice of two restaurants, both serving excellent meals. The Mantarae has a sophisticated menu and wine list, while the Bistro is a more casual affair.

SUVA

Bad Dog Café $$ *219 Victoria Parade, at MacArthur Sreet, Suva, tel: 331 2884.* The word 'café' may be a bit of a misnomer, as this is one of Suva's most popular small pubs, where expatriate residents meet for a drink or a meal after work. Main courses include char-grilled steaks, marinated yellow-fin tuna and pizzas.

Capital Palace Restaurant $–$$ *54 Victoria Parade, Suva, tel: 331 6088.* A Chinese restaurant with the expected décor.

Hare Krishna Restaurant $$ *16 Pratt Street, Suva, tel: 331 4154.* This restaurant, and another on Cumming Street, are managed by the Hare Krishna sect. They serve great vegetarian food and 'the best ice cream in town'. No smoking or alcohol allowed.

J.J.'s On the Park $$ *Stinson Parade, Suva, tel: 330 5005*. Choice Western-style meals for those missing home, with excellent water-front views and wireless Internet connection.

Old Mill Cottage $ *47–49 Carnavon Sreet, near corner of Loftus Street, Suva, tel: 331 2134*. This quaint, late 19th-century building, located in Suva's diplomatic-government section of town, has cafeteria-style counters which serve an excellent choice of European, Fijian and Indian foods. Look for the daily specials. No reservations. Cash only.

L'Opera Ristorante Italiano $$$ *59 Gordon Street, Suva, tel: 331 8602*. This restaurant's authentic Italian menu changes regularly. A fixed-price lunch is available on weekdays and at Sunday brunch. Some have called this 'Suva's most refined dining'. Open for lunch and dinner. Reservations recommended.

Republic of Cappuccino aka The ROC $ *Loftus Street, off Victoria Parade and 9 Renwick Street, Suva, tel: 999 7719*. The only coffee-house chain in Fiji, ROC specialises in espresso beverages and is also famous for its smoothies. There's a good selection of sandwiches, cakes, panini, sausage rolls and other café fare. Internet access.

SUNSHINE COAST

The Back Yard Café $–$$ *Vuda Point Marina, Lautoka, tel: 666 8214, email: <vudamarina@connect.com.fj>*. A welcoming café with light snacks and meals and great coffee.

Chand's Restaurant $–$$ *Upstairs on the main street, Ba*. Serves Chinese, Indian, European and Fijian cuisine. Consider carefully the strength of any curry you order: 'mild' can be very spicy indeed.

Lautoka Regent Café $ *15 Naviti Street, Lautoka, tel: 664 0282*. Conveniently situated beside an ATM, the café is air-conditioned and has Internet access. Try the sandwiches or fresh salads from the F$5 salad bar. Good coffee from F$3.20, hot and cold light meals, plus fruit smoothies, pies and pastries.

MAMANUCAS, YASAWAS AND KADAVU

If you're staying at a resort on the Mamanucas or Yasawas, or on Kadavu, there is little choice of eateries unless you go to another resort – if there is one on your island. However, resorts generally serve a good variety of food to a high standard. Meal plans are usually available.

OVALAU

Paak Kum Loong $ *Beach Street, Levuka, tel: 344 0059*. This Chinese-style restaurant is open for lunch and dinner, and also serves excellent Indian dishes. There's a balcony where you can sit and watch the languid activity of the town.

Whale's Tale Restaurant $ *Beach Street, Levuka, tel: 344 0234*. Centrally located in Levuka, and with ocean-themed décor, this restaurant serves healthy-sized helpings of European food.

VANUA LEVU

SAVUSAVU

Bula Re Café $–$$ *On the main street, Savusavu, tel: 885 0377*. German-and Fijian-owned, this café serves up breakfast, lunch and dinner from a menu that includes omelettes, crêpes, soup, salad, fish, chicken and beef, as well as desserts. Look for the daily specials. Every Wednesday is a *lovo* night.

Captain's Café $–$$ *Copra Shed Marina, Savusavu, tel: 885 0511*. Serves great breakfasts, lunches and dinners. Choose from seafood salad, sandwiches, pizza, fish, steak and chicken, plus daily specials. The café has a fabulous location, from where diners can sit and watch the harbour activity.

Cruisers $$ *Copra Shed Marina, Savusavu, tel: 885 3555*. Cruisers serves authentic Japanese cuisine, including sushi and sashimi. Food is of a high standard and is reasonably priced.

Planters' Club $–$$ *On the main street, Savusavu, tel: 885 0233.* A relic from the colonial era, the Planters' Club was once the domain of the region's plantation owners. Today, it's a welcoming place to meet people and hear the local news over a drink or light meal. On Sundays there's a traditional Fijian *lovo*.

Sea View Café $ *On the main street, Savusavu, tel: 885 0106.* The Sea View has a bright, cheerful interior with a *bure*-style bar and shaded outdoor veranda. Popular with visiting yachtsmen, the café serves great traditional Fijian, Indian and some European dishes, everything from fish and chips to chow mein.

TAVEUNI

Audrey's Sweet Somethings $ *Matei, Taveuni, tel: 888 0039.* Audrey Brown is a delightful American who fell in love with Taveuni years ago and couldn't leave. She serves home-made *kahlua,* cake and Fijian coffee on her shady veranda overlooking the sea. Eating here is a classic experience, so allow time to linger. Open daily for cake, coffee and tea.

Coconut Grove Beachfront Cottages $$–$$$ *9 Matei Road, tel: 888 0328.* Diners at this intimate resort restaurant are served their meals on the owners' veranda, which overlooks the sea. On some nights, a Fijian group sings and plays ukuleles, and there are beach *meke* and *lovo* nights. Great home-made pasta, curries and New Zealand beef. Open for breakfast, lunch and dinner.

Restaurant Tramonto $$ *Matei Road, tel: 888 2224.* A small restaurant in a spectacular setting that is extremely popular, so it's advisable to make a reservation. Special evenings for buffets, BBQs and lobster.

Vunibokoi Restaurant $$ *at Tovutovu Resort on the edge of Naselesele Village, near Matei airstrip, tel: 888 0560.* This resort restaurant serves Fijian dishes with a gourmet touch, using ingredients from its own organic gardens. The menu changes regularly, but seafood is a perennial speciality.

INDEX